Sunbonnet Sue
is Alive
& Well

American School of Needlework®, Inc.
San Marcos, California

Bobbie Matela, Managing Editor
Carol Wilson Mansfield, Art Director
Linda Causee, Editor
Meredith Montross, Associate Editor
Christina Wilson, Assistant Editor
Terea Mitchell, Illustrations
Graphic Solutions, inc-chgo, Book Design

©1995 by American School of Needlework®, Inc.; ASN Publishing, 1455 Linda Vista Drive, San Marcos, CA 92069

ISBN: 0-88195-737-2   Printed in U.S.A.   3 4 5 6 7 8 9

Introduction

Nobody doesn't like Sunbonnet Sue! Sunbonnet Sue and her pal Overall Sam are without a doubt the two best-known characters in the quilt world. Despite their longevity, Sue's enemies have been reporting her demise for years. Some of them have even tried to kill her in most atrocious ways. Others have attempted to have poor Sue make political statements.

We happen to like Sue!

We asked the Friends of Sue (sixteen quilt designers) to create quilts that show Sue at her best. Each quilter was given the same patterns and asked to put Sue in a setting befitting her station in the quilt world. No political statements, no attempts to make Sue do evil deeds–just Sue (and Sam) in charming settings.

The quilters were given the same rules:

1. Design an interesting setting and arrangement for Sue and Sam in sizes ranging from mini to crib.

2. Use the appliqué patterns provided in 3", 5", and 7" heights.

Patterns could be flopped, but the quilters were not permitted to change the size.

While they all began with the same tools, each of the quilters did her (or his) own thing, and the results were diverse and original. Each quilter seemed to gravitate to that process which most appealed to her (or him). Myrna Giesbrecht insisted upon rows and rows of fine machine quilting; Marti Michell (who was so intrigued by the assignment that she made two quilts) let her fabrics tell the story in each block of her calendar quilt; Marinda Stewart created Sue's garden from silk ribbon; Lesly-Claire Greenberg set Sue in a quilt show complete with stanchions and roping in front of a perfectly created miniature Log Cabin quilt; while Ellen Rosintoski used her favorite method of foundation piecing to take Sue on a path of miniature quilt blocks through the park. Nancy Brenan Daniel used rapid and traditional piecing techniques to make a strawberry garden for her Sue; Bettina Havig gave her Sue the traditional values of a home

with her Sam and a white picket fence; Dori Hawks chose hand-dyed fabrics and sneakers to adorn her Sue; Meredith Montross made her Sue disappear in the stars, and Bobbie Matela used quiltmaking as an opportunity to talk about her own life at ASN Publishing; Carol Wilson Mansfield, who in her position as Art Director of ASN had photographed countless angels, could not resist turning Sue into an angel. Clydene Sigle put her Sue in the same foundation-pieced pineapple blocks that had won her prizes. Linda Causee created an Irish Chain for her Sue; Anita Murphy's quilt reflects memories of her own life, and our one male quilter, Kim De Coste, of course, forgot Sue and made Sam the star of his quilt.

Yes, Sunbonnet Sue is truly alive and well!

Rita Weiss

Rita Weiss

Table of Contents

Special Techniques

Foundation Piecing

Some of the quilts in this book use Foundation Piecing. It is a wonderful method for piecing small or unusual pieces. It may take a little more time to do because of tracing the block patterns onto muslin or paper, but the accuracy it provides makes Foundation Piecing well worth the effort.

There are two ways to transfer a block pattern onto a fabric or paper foundation:

a. Trace block, centered on a muslin or paper square using a permanent marking pen. If you are unable to see the design through the fabric or paper, use a light source such as a light box, window or glass top table with a light under it.

b. Trace block onto paper using a transfer pen or pencil. Transfer block onto muslin or paper using an iron and following manufacturer's directions.

If you use method b, be sure to note that if block is not entirely symmetrical, it will appear as the mirror image to the photographed model. If it doesn't matter as to the overall design of the quilt, trace block as described. If it does matter, you must first trace the block onto tracing paper with a fine black marker. Turn paper over and trace wrong side of paper using a transfer pen or pencil. Transfer onto paper or muslin following manufacturer's directions.

Detailed instructions for Foundation Piecing are given with the individual quilts, *Sunbonnets' Shoes* by Dori Hawks, page 31, *Sunday in the Park with Sunbonnet Sue* by Ellen Rosintoski, page 52, *Pineapple Sue and Sam* by Clydene Sigle, page 17, and *Sunbonnet Sue At the Quilt Show* by Lesly-Claire Greenberg, page 57, as different designers have their own technique for using this method.

Using Templates

The quilts in this collection require patterns for piecing and appliqué; in quilting, patterns are called "templates."

Note: The template patterns for piecing are printed with seam allowance. The patterns for appliqué are printed without seam allowance.

To make templates for piecing, lay a piece of tracing paper over the pattern pieces in the book and carefully trace the pattern pieces. For hand piecing, trace pattern along dashed line and add 1/4" seam allowance all around when cutting from fabric. For machine piecing, trace pattern along solid line and use a consistent 1/4" seam allowance when sewing. (Do not photocopy the pieces instead of tracing. Photocopy machines are not exact, and your pieces may not fit together.) Carefully glue your tracing onto heavy cardboard or plastic. Special plastic for making templates is available in quilt, craft or stationery stores. If you use a clear plastic, you can trace directly onto plastic and eliminate the gluing.

Once you have made your template, carefully cut it out. It is important that your templates be cut out carefully because if they are not accurate, the patchwork will not fit together. Use a pair of good-size sharp scissors (not the same scissors that you use to cut fabric), a single-edged razor blade or a craft knife. Be careful not to bend the corners of the triangles.

Hold your pencil or marker at an angle so that the point is against the side of the template and trace around the template onto fabric. Continue moving the template and tracing it on fabric the required number of times, moving from left to right and always keeping straight lines parallel with grain.

You can use your rotary cutter to cut several layers at once. Fold fabric so you have as many layers as the number of pieces needed. Lay your template on the wrong side of the fabric which has been folded. Place it so that as many straight sides of the piece as possible are parallel to the crosswise and lengthwise grain of the fabric. Now trace around the template. Then use your acrylic ruler and rotary cutter along the traced lines, making certain that you cut away from your body.

Appliqué Techniques

Traditional Basting Method

1. Trace pattern piece on right side of fabric and mark around the piece, using the proper marking tool. In some of the quilts, Sunbonnet Sue and Overall Sam are facing each other. Note the direction and trace pattern pieces facing that direction. Measure 1/4" around the shape and draw a second line. This second line is your cutting line. As you become more proficient, you will be able to add this 1/4" seam allowance purely by eye.

2. Cut shape out of fabric with a good sharp scissors.

3. Turn under seam allowance and finger press the turned-under edges in place. Baste the edges as you turn them, keeping your finger pressing about an inch ahead of the needle. The thread that you use for basting should be enough of a contrast so that you can see the thread for removal when the appliqué is finally attached. However, it is best not to use a dark-colored thread on light fabric as this may leave some marking when the basting is removed. *Note: Edges which fit underneath other pieces do not need to have seam allowances turned under.*

4. A concave curve (curve that goes inward) should be clipped so that the

seam allowance will flatten when turned under, **Fig 1**. Make as few clips as possible because the cutting can cause the fabric to fray. Clip curves only as you come to them to prevent fraying.

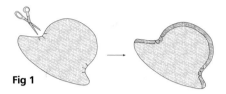

Fig 1

Hint: Make a few cuts, then turn under the seam allowance and check to see how flat the piece is lying. If the edge is not flat enough, make a few more cuts.

Convex curves are never clipped. A convex curve is an edge that goes outward from the shape.

5. Pin each piece into place and, if desired, baste onto the quilt block. Pieces which fit under other pieces should be placed down first. When entire block is pinned or basted in place, sew pieces to block using a blind stitch seen in **Fig 2**. Go up at **A**, catching one or two threads of folded appliqué piece; go back down at **B** into background fabric (quilt top), next to fold. Come back up through background about 1/8" away at **C**, catching one to two threads into folded appliqué. Continue around entire piece.

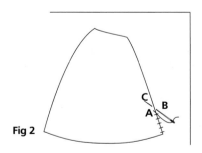

Fig 2

Freezer Paper Method

1. Trace the number of pattern pieces needed as listed in individual projects onto dull side of freezer paper; cut out along traced line. *Note:* Trace pattern pieces in the direction that you want

them to face on your quilt. For example, if Sunbonnet Sue will face left on your quilt, trace pattern pieces facing left.

2. Place freezer paper pieces shiny side up on wrong side of desired fabric; cut out pattern pieces adding 1/8" to 1/4" seam allowance all around.

3. Fold seam allowance over freezer paper toward shiny side; press edge with hot, dry iron, **Fig 3**. If there is a pointed tip on an appliqué piece, fold edge at tip first, **Fig 4**, then continue folding and pressing.

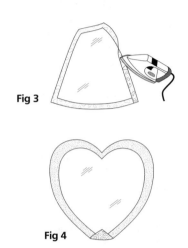

Fig 3

Fig 4

4. Place appliqué piece in position on quilt top; baste or pin in place. Stitch appliqué piece in place using blind stitch.

5. Cut a small slit in background behind appliqué piece; remove freezer paper.

Freezer Paper with School Paste Method

1. Trace the number of pattern pieces needed as listed in individual projects onto dull side of freezer paper; cut out along traced line. *Note:* Trace pattern pieces in the opposite direction that you want them to face on your quilt. For example, if Sunbonnet Sue will face left on your quilt, trace pattern pieces facing right.

2. Place freezer paper pieces shiny side down on wrong side of fabric; press in place. Cut out pattern pieces adding 1/8" to 1/4" seam allowance all around.

3. Spread thin layer of school paste along seam allowance, **Fig 5**. *Hint:* Have a wet paper towel handy to wipe sticky fingers as you do this step.

Fig 5

4. Fold pasty seam allowance onto freezer paper; let dry completely.

5. Place appliqué piece in position on quilt top; baste or pin in place. Stitch appliqué piece in place using blind stitch.

6. After the appliqué is finished, wet the whole square, cut a small slit in the back of the appliqué and pull out the freezer paper with tweezers or a set of hemostats. *Note: If you have not pre-washed the fabrics or tested for color fastness, do not wet the entire piece. Take an ice cube and wet just the edges to loosen the glue and pull away the freezer paper.*

Spray Starch Method

1. Trace one of each pattern piece needed for your project onto thin cardboard such as posterboard.

2. Trace the number of pattern pieces needed onto wrong side of fabric. *Note: Trace pattern pieces in the opposite direction that you want them to face on your quilt. For example, if Sunbonnet Sue will face left on your quilt, trace pattern pieces facing right.* Cut out leaving a 1/8" to 1/4" seam allowance all around.

3. Place cardboard template on wrong side of fabric.

4. Spray a small amount of spray starch in a small dish; "paint" spray starch onto seam allowance using a small paint brush or a cotton swab, **Fig 6**. Try not to get the template wet.

Fig 6

continued

5. Fold wet edges over cardboard template and hold iron on seam allowance until dry, **Fig 7**.

Fig 7

6. Turn template over and iron fabric on right side. Remove cardboard template.

7. Place appliqué piece in position on quilt top; baste or pin in place. Stitch appliqué piece in place using Blind Stitch.

Appliqué with Fusible Interfacing

1. Make templates as described in Using Templates, page 4.

2. Trace number of pattern pieces needed for your project onto wrong side of fabric. *Note: Trace pattern pieces in the opposite direction that you want them to face on your quilt. For example, if Sunbonnet Sue will face left on your quilt, trace pattern pieces facing right.*

3. Cut pattern pieces out leaving a 1/8" to 1/4" seam allowance all around.

4. Trace the same number of pattern pieces facing the opposite direction of the fabric pieces onto non-fusible side of fusible interfacing. Cut out leaving a 1/8" to 1/4" seam allowance all around.

5. Place interfacing piece right (non-fusible) side up on right side of a fabric piece. Stitch around entire piece, **Fig 8**.

Fig 8

6. Cut a small slit in interfacing layer only, **Fig 9**. Turn piece right side out. Use a point turner or hemostat to smooth edges. Finger press edges.

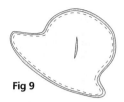

Fig 9

7. Prepare all pieces in same manner.

8. Place pieces in position on quilt top. When you are satisfied with placement, iron in place. Stitch around all edges using a hand blind stitch or decorative machine stitching. Clydene Sigle used a machine Blanket Stitch to appliqué in *Pineapple Sue and Sam*, page 17.

Appliqué with Lining Fabric

1. Follow steps 1 to 7 in Appliqué with Fusible Interfacing above to prepare pieces for appliqué, except replace interfacing with a lining fabric.

2. If you are doing several pieces of the same fabric, trace them onto wrong side of fabric, leaving space between each piece for seam allowance. Sew to lining fabric before cutting and turning as described in *Sunbonnet Angel*, page 22.

3. Place pieces in position on quilt top. When you are satisfied with placement, pin or baste in place. Stitch around all edges using a hand blind stitch or decorative machine stitching.

4. As described in *Friends Forever*, page 65, you may leave some of the appliqué pieces "loose," such as Sue's apron to give added dimension.

Appliqué with Paper-backed Fusible Webbing

1. Trace number of pattern pieces needed for your project onto paper side of fusible webbing, making sure pieces are facing the opposite direction that they will face on your quilt.

Note: If you are making several pieces that will be from the same fabric, trace together on the fusible webbing, **Fig 10**.

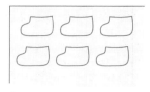

Fig 10

2. Place fusible webbing (paper side up) on wrong side of fabric. Cut out along traced line. You do not have to leave a seam allowance around pieces. Fuse in place following manufacturer's directions. Remove paper backing.

3. Place appliqué pieces in position on quilt top. Tap each piece with a hot iron as you position it to keep it in place until all pieces are positioned.

4. When you are satisfied with placement, fuse pieces in place following manufacturer's directions.

5. Stitch around edges using a machine zigzag or other decorative stitch. Ellen Rosintoski used metallic thread and a machine zigzag to add some sparkle to Sue in *Sunday in the Park with Sunbonnet Sue,* page 52.

Appliquéing Sue and Sam

There are three different heights of Sunbonnet Sue and Overall Sam that were used in the collection of quilts in this book, 3", 5" and 7". There is also a variation of the largest size, with Sam being slightly taller with smaller Shoes and Sue having a longer Dress and smaller Shoes. Placement Diagrams for each size of Sunbonnet Sue and Overall Sam as well as pattern pieces for each size are found on pages 72 to 77.

Once you have prepared your pieces for appliqué using one of the Appliqué Techniques (except Appliqué with Paper-backed Fusible Webbing) described above, you are ready to appliqué Sue or Sam to your background fabric.

1. To make placement easier, trace Placement Diagram of Sue or Sam in the size you are using onto template plastic; trace along all solid lines.

Position Sue or Sam onto your background fabric and trace around shape.

2. For Sue, **Fig 11**, place Shoe in position on background first. Next, place Dress on background with lower edge of Dress covering upper edge of Shoe, then place Apron on top of Dress, with neck and front edges even. Position Bonnet over neck edge of Dress and Apron and finally, place Sleeve on top of Apron just under Bonnet; tuck Hand under lower edge of Sleeve. When all pieces are in position, place template with traced lines over it to check; pin in place. Appliqué along all edges as explained in your chosen technique directions.

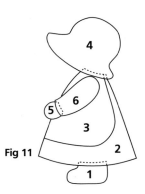

Fig 11

3. For Sam, **Fig 12**, place Shoe in position on background first. Place Shirt on background, then position Overalls over Shirt making sure that lower edge of Overalls covers top edge of Shoe.

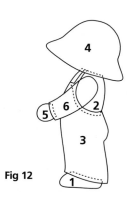

Fig 12

Position Hat with lower edge covering top edge of Shirt. Place Arm on Shirt just below Hat, tucking Hand under lower edge of Sleeve. When all pieces are in position, place template with traced lines over it to check; pin in place. Appliqué along all edges as explained in your chosen technique directions.

Finishing Your Quilt

Adding Borders

Although measurements for border strips are given, we recommend that before cutting your border strips, you measure the finished quilt top and cut borders to the exact size. If you have made some mistakes in the piecing (for instance, if you made your blocks with a larger than 1/4" seam allowance) this will be the time to adjust border measurements.

Using the 1/4" seam allowance, attach one side border to the right side of the quilt and one to the left. Then attach the top and bottom borders. Use the 1/4" seam allowance at all times. Repeat for additional borders.

Preparing the Quilt Top

Give the quilt top a final blocking, making sure all corners are square and all seams are pressed to one side.

We have made suggestions for quilting your quilt, but you may wish to follow your own quilting plan. However if you are planning to quilt your top, you will need to mark the quilting pattern before joining the top to the batting and backing.

If you prefer to tie your quilt, skip the next section on marking the quilting design.

Marking the Quilting Design

Before marking on your quilt top, be sure to test any marking material to make sure it will wash out of your fabric. Mark all quilting lines on the right side of the fabric. For marking, use a hard lead pencil, chalk or other special quilt marking materials. If you quilt right on the marked lines, they will not show.

A word of caution: Marking lines which are intended to disappear after quilting - either by exposure to air or with water - may become permanent when set with a hot iron. Therefore, don't iron your quilt top after you have marked your quilting pattern.

If you are quilting around shapes, you may not need to mark your line if you feel that you can accurately gauge the quilting line as you work. If you are quilting "in the ditch" of the seam (the space right in the seam), marking is not necessary. Other quilting patterns will need to be marked.

Attaching Batting and Backing

There are a number of different types of batting on the market. Very thin batting will require a great deal of quilting to hold it (quilting lines no more than 1" apart); very thick batting should be used only for tied quilts.

If you are planning to machine quilt, you should investigate the new battings on the market which are intended for machine quilting.

We have indicated the amount of fabric required for the backing in each pattern. If you prefer another fabric, buy a backing fabric that is soft and loosely woven so that the quilting needle can pass through easily. Bed sheets are usually not good backing materials.

Since some of the quilts in this book are wider than fabric width, you will have to sew lengths together to make your quilt backing. Cut off selvages and seam pieces together carefully; iron seam open. This is the only time in making a quilt that seams should be pressed open.

Cut batting and backing larger than the quilt top; about 2" wider than quilt top on all sides. Place backing, wrong side up, on flat surface. Place batting on top of this, matching outer edges.

continued

Hint: Remove batting from its packaging a day in advance and open it out full size. This will help the batting to lie flat.

The layers of the quilt must be held together before quilting. There are two methods for doing this: thread basting and safety pin basting.

For thread basting: First, place backing wrong side up, then batting; center quilt top, right side up, on top of the batting. Baste with long stitches, starting in the center and sewing toward the edges in a number of diagonal lines.

For safety pin basting: Layer the backing, batting and quilt top and pin through all three layers at once. Because you don't have to put your hand under the quilt as you do when you are thread basting, the quilt top does not move out of position. Start pinning from center and work out to edges, placing pins no more than 4" to 6" apart. Think of your quilt plan as you work and make certain that your pins avoid prospective quilting lines. Choose rustproof pins that are size #1 or #2. To make pinning easier, many quilters use a quilter's spoon. The spoon is notched, so that it can push the point of the safety pin closed.

Quilting

The quilts in this collection can be hand or machine quilted. If you have never used a sewing machine for quilting, you might want to read some more about the technique. *Quilting for People Who Don't Have Time to Quilt* (Book #4111) by Marti Michell and *A Beginner's Guide to Machine Quilting* (Book #4121) by Judi Tyrrell, both published by ASN Publishing, are excellent introductions to machine quilting. These books are available at your local quilt store or department, or write the publisher for a list of sources.

You do not need a special machine for quilting. You can machine quilt with almost any home sewing machine. Just make sure that it is in good working order and that the presser foot is not set for too much pressure which can cause rippling. An even-feed foot is a good investment if you are going to machine quilt since it feeds the top and bottom layers through the machine evenly.

Use fine transparent nylon thread in the top and regular sewing thread in the bobbin.

To **quilt-in-the-ditch** of a seam (this is actually stitching in the space between two pieces of fabric that have been sewn together), use your hands to pull the blocks or pieces apart and machine stitch right between the two pieces. Try to keep your stitching just to the side of the seam that does not have the bulk of the seam allowance under it. When you have finished stitching, the quilting will be practically hidden in the seam.

Free form machine quilting is done with a darning foot and the feed dogs down on your sewing machine. It can be used to quilt around a design or to quilt a motif. Mark your quilting design as described in Marking the Quilting Design on page 7. Free form machine quilting takes practice to master because you are controlling the quilt through the machine rather than the machine moving the quilt. With free form machine quilting you can quilt in any direction—up and down, side to side and even in circles without pivoting the quilt around the needle.

Attaching the Binding

Place the quilt on a flat surface and carefully trim the backing and batting 1/2" beyond the quilt top edge. Measure the quilt top and cut two 2"-wide (or width specified with quilt directions) binding strips the length of your quilt (for sides). Right sides together, sew one side strip to one side of the quilt with 1/4" seam allowance (seam allowance should be measured from outer edge of quilt top fabric, not outer edge of batting/backing). Turn binding to back and turn under 1/4" on raw edge; slipstitch to backing. Do other side in same manner. For top and bottom edge binding strips, measure carefully adding 1/2" to each end; cut strips 2" wide. To eliminate raw edges at corners, turn the extra 1/2" to wrong side before stitching to top and bottom. Finish in same manner as sides.

Sue's Album of Quilts

Friends Forever by Anita Murphy

Sunday in the Park
with Sunbonnet Sue
by Ellen Rosintoski

Sunbonnet Sue has
a Picket Fence
by Bettina Havig

Lost in the Stars
by Meredith Montross

Strawberries and Cream by Nancy Brenan Daniel

Sunbonnets' Shoes
by Dori Hawks

Sunbonnet Sue is Alive and Well
at The American School
of Needlework®
by Bobbie Matela

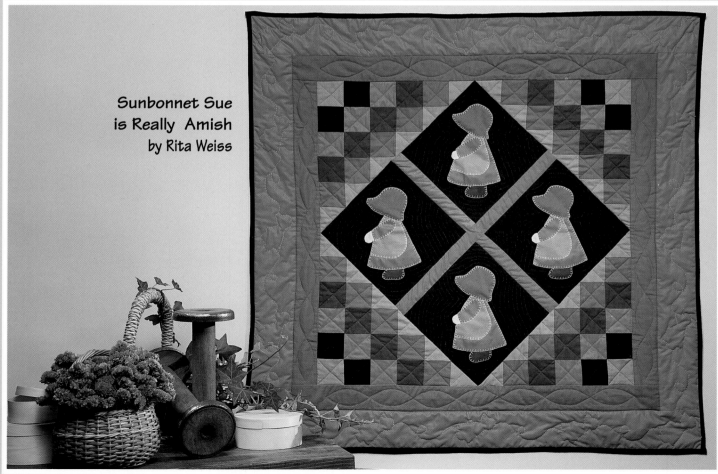

Sunbonnet Sue
is Really Amish
by Rita Weiss

Sunbonnet Sue in the Garden
by Marinda Stewart

Sunbonnet Sue at the Quilt Show
by Lesly-Claire Greenberg

Black Tie
by Kim DeCoste

Sunbonnet Angels
by Carol Wilson Mansfield

The Stars of Today's Show by Myrna Giesbrecht

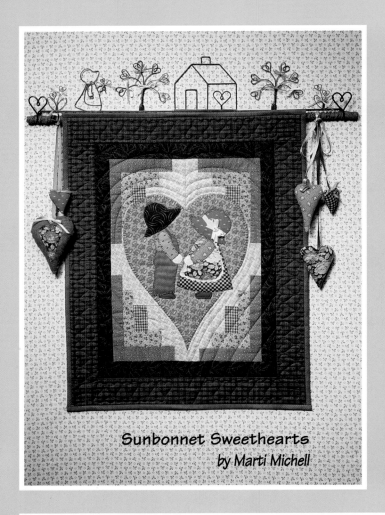

Sunbonnet Sweethearts
by Marti Michell

Friendship Chain
by Linda Causee

Pineapple Sunbonnet Sue
and Overall Sam
by Clydene Sigle

Pineapple Sue and Sam

by Clydene Sigle
San Diego, California

APPROXIMATE SIZE: 37" X 37"

The arrival of Clydene's first grand-daughter sparked her interest in Sunbonnet Sue. Clydene feels that every girl can find a place in her heart for Sue. This is her third quilt made using 3" Pineapple Blocks. One of her award-winning quilts was featured in Log Cabin Quilt Show *published by ASN Publishing.*

Fabric Requirements:

1 yd dk blue
1/3 yd tan print
3/8 yd each lt mauve, lt blue
1/2 yd each med mauve, med blue
1/4 yd dk mauve
1/3 yd med green
1 yd large floral print
2/3 yd muslin
1/3 yd off-white
1 1/4 yds backing fabric
45" square batting
optional: 1/2 yd lightweight fusible
   interfacing

Additional Supplies:
permanent fabric marker

Pattern Pieces (pages 73, 76 and 80):
7" Sunbonnet Sue
7" Overall Sam

Cutting Requirements:
Notes: Strips are cut on the crosswise (selvage to selvage) grain. Choose your favorite method of appliqué from Appliqué Techniques (pages 4 to 7) before cutting Sunbonnet Sue and Overall Sam pieces from fabric.

45 - 4" x 4" squares, muslin
   (foundation)
four 9 1/2" x 9 1/2" squares,
   off-white print (background)
*one 7/8"-wide strip, tan print
   (center squares)
*34 - 7/8"-wide strips, dk blue
   (strips 2, 4, 6, 8,10)
*ten 7/8"-wide strips each, lt blue and
   lt mauve (strips 3, 5, 7)

*twelve 7/8"-wide strips each, med
   blue and med mauve (strips 9, 11, 12)
two 1 1/4"-wide strips, large floral
   print (pieced triangles)
one 1 1/4"-wide strip each, med green,
   dk mauve, lt mauve, tan print,
   dk blue and lt blue (pieced triangles)
four 1 1/4"-wide strips, tan fabric
   (first border)
four 1 3/4"-wide strips, green fabric
   (second border)
four 4"-wide strips, floral print
   (third border)
four 2 1/2"-wide strips, floral print
   (binding)
one 7" Sunbonnet Sue and one
   reversed, desired fabrics
one 7" Overall Sam and one reversed,
   desired fabrics
*You may sew, then cut strips as you
   piece the Pineapple Blocks, or cut
   strips into the following lengths:

Shown in full color on page 16.

Piece#	Length	#of each Piece	Fabric
1	7/8"	45	tan print
2	1"	180	dk blue
3	1 1/4"	90	lt blue and lt mauve
4	1 1/4"	180	dk blue
5	1 1/2"	90	lt blue and lt mauve
6	1 1/2"	180	dk blue
7	1 3/4"	90	lt blue and lt mauve
8	1 7/8"	180	dk blue
9	2"	90	med blue and med mauve
10	2 1/8"	180	dk blue
11	2 1/8"	90	med blue and med mauve
12	1 1/4"	90	med blue and med mauve

Instructions:

Pineapple Blocks
Note: Read Foundation Piecing, page 4, before you begin.

1. Trace Pineapple Block Layout (page 80) onto each 4" muslin square for foundation.

continued

2. Place piece #1 (tan print) on unmarked side of foundation making sure that piece overlaps all marked sides of space #1, **Fig 1**; use a glue stick or pin to hold in place. *Note: The unmarked side of the foundation is the right side.*

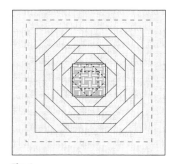

Fig 1

3. Place piece #2 (or strip) over piece #1 right sides together, **Fig 2**.

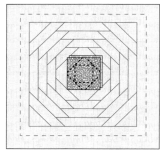

using cut pieces

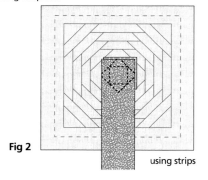

Fig 2

using strips

4. Carefully turn over foundation; stitch on marked line between marked #1 and #2, beginning and ending two stitches beyond line, **Fig 3**. Turn foundation to right side.

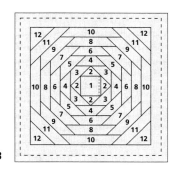

Fig 3

18

5. Fold foundation fabric back along seam just sewn and trim seam allowance to 1/8", **Fig 4**.

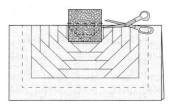

Fig 4

6. If using strip, trim even with piece #1, **Fig 5**.

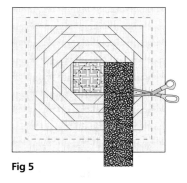

Fig 5

7. Fold open piece #2 and finger press; pin or glue in place, **Fig 6**.

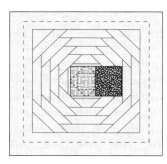

Fig 6

8. Repeat steps 3 to 7 with remaining three #2 pieces, **Fig 7**.

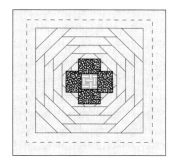

Fig 7

9. Fold muslin foundation back along next stitching line (between #2 and #3); trim seam allowance to 1/8", **Fig 8**.

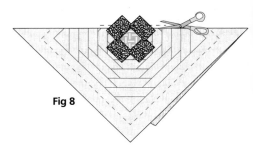

Fig 8

10. Repeat steps 3 to 9 for pieces 3 to 12 in numerical order, adding all pieces to right side and stitching from wrong (marked) side.

11. Press finished block; trim if necessary.

12. Repeat for all 45 blocks. There will be 14 blue blocks, 14 pink blocks, 16 half-pink/half-blue blocks and one block with blue in opposite corners/pink in opposite corners, **Fig 9**.

make 14

make 14

make 16

Fig 9

make 1

Sunbonnet Sue and Overall Sam Blocks

1. Draw four lines spaced 1/2" apart in each corner on wrong side of 9 1/2" square, **Fig 10**.

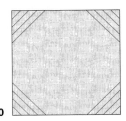

Fig 10

2. Using Foundation Piecing, place the first strip right side down on the unmarked side of block outside the first marked line, making sure it overlaps the line by 1/4", **Fig 11**.

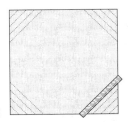

Fig 11

3. Turn block over to stitch from the wrong (marked) side. Fold strip over seam allowance and finger press in place; cut off strip even with block. Continue sewing three remaining strips in same manner.

4. Sew strips to remaining corners on all four squares, **Fig 12**. Square up blocks if necessary.

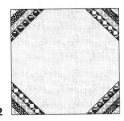

Fig 12

5. Refer to Appliqué Techniques, pages 6 and 7, to appliqué Sunbonnet Sue and Overall Sam pieces in the center of the 9 1/2" off-white squares. Photographed quilt was appliquéd using the Interfacing Method.

6. Appliqué around each piece using a Blanket Stitch, **Fig 13**.

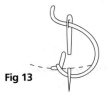

Fig 13

Finishing

1. Place blocks according to layout on page 17. Sew blocks together in rows, then sew rows together. *Hint: Use a scant 1/4" seam allowance when joining the Pineapple blocks due to the extra bulk of the muslin foundation.*

2. Measure width of quilt; cut two tan print border strips to that length. Sew to sides of quilt top.

3. Measure length of quilt including borders; cut two tan print strips to that length. Sew to top and bottom of quilt.

4. Repeat steps 2 and 3 for remaining two borders.

5. Layer quilt backing wrong side up, then batting, and quilt top right side up. Baste by hand or with safety pins. Quilt as desired. Photographed quilt was quilted in the ditch between borders and pieced triangle corners of Sue and Sam blocks. Two lines of quilting spaced 3/8" apart extend into the Sue and Sam blocks. An X was quilted through each Pineapple Block.

6. Refer to Attaching the Binding, page 8, to bind your quilt.

Sunbonnet Sue is Really Amish

by Rita Weiss
Escondido, California

APPROXIMATE SIZE: 34" X 34"

Because traditional Amish dolls are always faceless–choosing to hide their visages behind a black sunbonnet–Rita decided that Sue was probably really Amish and shows her in a traditional Amish quilt. Since the hallmark of an Amish quilt is its elaborate quilting especially in the borders, Rita has added quilted Sunbonnet Sues to her border. When she's not creating quilts, Rita serves as Executive Vice President of ASN Publishing.

Fabric Requirements:

2 yds black solid (background, backing and binding)
1/2 yd lt turquoise solid
1/2 yd dk turquoise solid
1/2 yd purple solid
1 yd fuchsia solid
scrap peach solid
42" square batting

Additional Supplies:

white perle cotton, size 5
template plastic
embroidery needle

Pattern Pieces (page 73):

7" Sunbonnet Sue

Quilting Patterns (page 88):

3" Sunbonnet Sue
Leaf
Wavy Line

Cutting Requirements:

Note: All strips are cut across the grain from selvage to selvage. Choose your favorite method of appliqué on pages 4 to 7 before cutting Sunbonnet Sue pattern pieces from fabric.
four of each 7" Sunbonnet Sue piece
four 8 1/4" squares, black
two 1 1/2" x 8 1/4" strips, fuchsia
one 1 1/2" x 17 1/4" strip, fuchsia
seven 2 1/2" x 10" strips, lt turquoise
five 2 1/2" x 10" strips, dk turquoise
four 2 1/2" x 10" strips, purple
three 2 1/2" x 10" strips, fuchsia
two 2 1/2" x 10" strips, black

Shown in full color on page 12.

two 2 1/2" x 24 1/2" strips, dk turquoise (first border)
two 2 1/2" x 28 1/2" strips, dk turquoise (first border)
two 3 1/2" x 28 1/2" strips, fuchsia (second border)
two 3 1/2" x 34 1/2" strips, fuchsia (second border)
four 2"-wide strips, black (binding)

Instructions:

Making the Pieced Corners

1. Sew 2 1/2" x 10" strips together as shown in **Fig 1**. You will have five different strip-pieced fabrics plus one lt turquoise strip. Press seams for each strip-pieced fabric in one direction, alternating direction from section to section.

2. Cut strip-pieced fabric crosswise every 2 1/2" and cut lt turquoise strip into 2 1/2" squares, **Fig 2**.

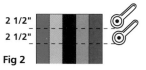

2 1/2"
2 1/2"
Fig 2

3. Sew pieces together to create a pieced corner, **Fig 3**; repeat for all four corners. Press seams in one direction.

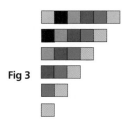

Fig 3

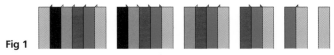

Fig 1

Making the Center Section

1. Referring to Appliqué Techniques, pages 4 to 7, use your favorite method to appliqué Sunbonnet Sue diagonally on each of four black squares, **Fig 4**.

Fig 4

2. Stitch around edges of all Sunbonnet Sue pieces with a Blanket Stitch, **Fig 5,** and white perle cotton.

Fig 5

3. Sew a Sunbonnet Sue block to each side of a 1 1/2" x 8 1/4" fuchsia strip, **Fig 6**; repeat.

Fig 6

4. Sew Sunbonnet Sue pairs to each side of 1 1/2" x 17 1/4" fuchsia strip, **Fig 7**, to complete center section. Press.

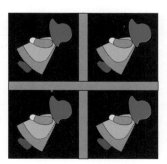

Fig 7

Finishing the Quilt

1. Place center section right sides together with corner section; be sure that raw edge of center section is even with inner corners of corner section, **Fig 8**.

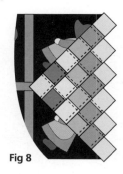

Fig 8

2. Trim excess corner fabric even with center section, **Fig 9**; repeat on remaining three sides.

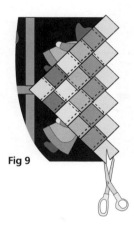

Fig 9

3. Repeat steps 1 and 2 on opposite side, then remaining two sides, **Fig 10**.

Fig 10

4. Sew dk turquoise strips to sides of quilt first, then top and bottom. Repeat for fuchsia border.

5. Referring to quilt layout, page 20, mark quilting design in borders using fabric pencil or water soluble marking pen. The Leaf pattern was quilted in the dk turquoise border; begin drawing in the center of each border, continuing pattern on each side. The 3" Sunbonnet Sue outline was quilted in the fuchsia border; draw one Sue in each corner with three more evenly spaced on each border. Add the looped line between each Sue. (See layout, page 20.)

6. Place backing wrong side up, then batting and quilt top right side up. Baste by hand or with safety pins. Quilt by hand or machine. Photographed quilt was machine quilted diagonally through the pieced corner squares and in the ditch between blocks and borders; lines spaced about 1/4" following Sue's shape were echo quilted in the black background squares. The Sunbonnet Sue design in the fuchsia border was hand quilted with white quilting thread.

7. Refer to Attaching the Binding, page 8, to attach binding.

Sunbonnet Angels

by Carol Wilson Mansfield
Rancho Bernardo, California

APPROXIMATE SIZE: 24" X 24"

When given the required pattern pieces for Sue, Carol turned the Apron piece, and it became an angel wing. The stars on Sue's Bonnet (her halo) are small gold-tone charms. Star-shaped sequins, buttons or beads could also be used. To complete her heavenly motif, Carol set her Angel Sue in a star setting. When she's not designing Sunbonnet Sues, Carol serves as the Art Director at ASN Publishing and is responsible for their prize-winning covers.

Fabric Requirements:

1 yd lt blue print (Star Squares and backing)
1/2 yd off-white print (Dress, Star Squares)
1/2 yd yellow print (Wings/Apron and Starry Border)
1/2 yd med blue print, (Sunbonnet Angel Blocks, binding)
1/2 yd dk blue print (Starry Border)
1/4 yd white (lining of appliqué pieces)
1/8 yd white print (Sleeve)
1/8 yd tan print (Bonnet)
1/8 yd peach (Hands and Shoes/Feet)
32" square batting

Pattern Pieces (page 72):
5" Sunbonnet Sue

Additional Supplies:
ball point bodkin, large tapestry needle or other blunt pointed tool
twenty gold star charms, about 3/8" across

Cutting Requirements:
Note: Read Sunbonnet Angel Blocks, page 23, or choose your favorite method of appliqué, pages 4 to 7, before cutting Sunbonnet Sue pieces from fabric.
one 2 7/8" x 23" strip, off-white print (Star Blocks)
one 2 7/8" x 23" strip, lt blue print (Star Blocks)

Shown in full color on page 14.

sixteen 2 1/2" squares, lt blue (Star Blocks)
four 2 1/2" squares, off-white print (Star Blocks)
five 6 1/2" squares, med blue print (Sunbonnet Angel Blocks)
two 2 7/8" x 41" strips, yellow print (Starry Border)
two 2 7/8" x 41" strips, dk blue print (Starry Border)
twelve 2 1/2" squares, dk blue print (Starry Border)
*four 2 1/2" x 27" strips, med blue print (binding)

*Measure your quilt and cut strips to that size plus 5".

Instructions:

Star Blocks

1. Draw 2 7/8" squares on wrong side of 2 7/8" x 23" off-white strip; draw diagonal lines through every square, **Fig 1**.

Fig 1

2. Place marked strip right sides together with 2 7/8" x 23" lt blue strip. Stitch 1/4" from diagonal line along both sides, **Fig 2**.

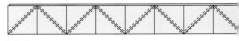

Fig 2

3. Cut along all drawn lines, **Fig 3**. Press seam toward darker fabric; clip dog ears, **Fig 4**.

Fig 3

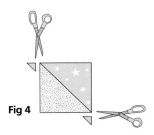

Fig 4

4. For rows 1 and 3, sew a pieced square on opposite sides of a 2 1/2" lt blue square, **Fig 5**; repeat.

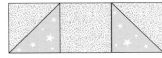

Fig 5

Rows 1 and 3

5. For row 2, sew a 2 1/2" lt blue square on each side of a 2 1/2" off-white square, **Fig 6**.

Fig 6

Row 2

6. Sew rows 1, 2 and 3 together to complete Star Block, **Fig 7**.

7. Repeat steps 4 to 6 for a total of four Star Blocks.

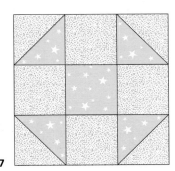

Fig 7

Sunbonnet Angel Blocks

1. Trace Bonnet five times onto wrong side of white lining fabric, leaving at least 1/2" space around each piece, **Fig 8**. *Note: Be sure to trace pattern pieces facing the opposite direction of finished block.*

Fig 8

2. Continue tracing pattern pieces onto wrong side of lining fabric, grouping five of each pattern piece onto the fabric, **Fig 9**. *Note: Group Hands and Shoes/Feet together since they will be made using the same fabric. Do not cut anything apart at this time.*

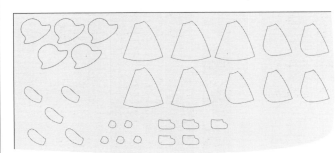

Fig 9

3. Position lining fabric over the right side of the desired pattern piece fabric; pin in place, **Fig 10**.

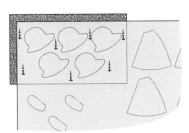

Fig 10

4. Using a very small stitch, stitch along drawn lines of Bonnet, **Fig 11**, then sew along drawn lines of Apron/Wing and Sleeve. As you finish stitching each group of pattern pieces, cut them off to make stitching the next group easier. Stitch along three sides of Hand, Shoe/Foot and Dress, **Fig 12**.

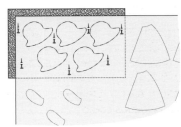

Fig 11

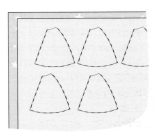

Fig 12

5. Cut out each individual piece about 1/8" from stitching, except for the open side of Hand, Dress and Shoe/Foot which should have a 1/4" seam allowance.

6. To finish Hand, Dress and Shoe/Foot pieces, turn inside out through the open side. Use a ball point bodkin, large tapestry needle or other blunt pointed tool to smooth the curves and push the stitched edge into shape. Press with main fabric facing up.

continued

7. To finish Apron/Wing, Bonnet, and Sleeve, make a small cut (about 1/2" to 1") in middle of lining fabric, **Fig 13**. Be sure to cut through **one layer only** and stay away from edge as far as possible. Using a blunt pointed tool, coax the main fabric through the cut, then smooth the curves and seams into shape; press smooth.

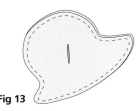

Fig 13

8. Position pieces on 6 1/2" med blue square, **Fig 14**; pin in place. *Note: Place Dress down first, positioning Shoe/Foot under Dress; place Apron/Wings, then Bonnet and finally Sleeve with Hand underneath. Attach appliqué pieces using a blind stitch.*

Fig 14

Finishing the Quilt

1. For Starry Border, draw 2 7/8" squares on wrong side of two yellow 2 7/8" x 41" strips; draw diagonal line through each square (see **Fig 1**).

2. Place yellow strips right sides together with dk blue strips; stitch 1/4" from each side of diagonal lines (see **Fig 2**).

3. Cut on all drawn lines; press seams toward darker fabric. Trim dog ears.

4. Sew a pieced square to opposite sides of a 2 1/2" dk blue square, **Fig 15**. Repeat for a total of twelve pieced strips.

Fig 15

5. Sew three pieced strips together end to end for side border; sew pieced square at each end, **Fig 16**. Repeat for one more side border.

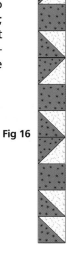

Fig 16

6. Place Sunbonnet Angel Blocks, Star Blocks, pieced strips and side borders according to **Fig 17**.

Fig 17

7. Sew blocks and pieced strips together in vertical rows, then sew rows together. Attach side borders.

8. Place binding strip right sides together with quilt top, making sure both ends extend about 2 1/2"; sew to within 1/4" of each end, **Fig 18**. Repeat on all four sides.

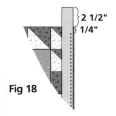

2 1/2"
1/4"

Fig 18

9. To miter corner, fold quilt top in half diagonally, extending binding straight out, **Fig 19**.

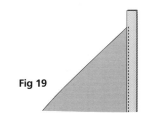

Fig 19

10. Sew binding strips at a 45 degree angle using the fold as a guide, **Fig 20**. *Hint: Draw line at 45 degree angle using fold as a guide, then stitch over line.* Trim excess fabric 1/4" from stitching, **Fig 21**. Repeat at remaining three corners.

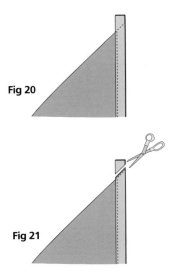

Fig 20

Fig 21

11. Place backing wrong side up on flat surface, then batting and quilt top right side up. Baste by hand or with safety pins.

12. Quilt as desired. Photographed quilt was quilted 1/4" from seam lines and in the ditch between blocks and binding.

13. Turn quilt over and trim batting and backing to 1/2" from edge of binding, **Fig 22**.

Fig 22

14. Fold binding 1 1/4" toward back of quilt. At corners, fold corners first, then sides, **Fig 23**. The batting will roll with the binding for a soft finish.

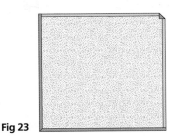

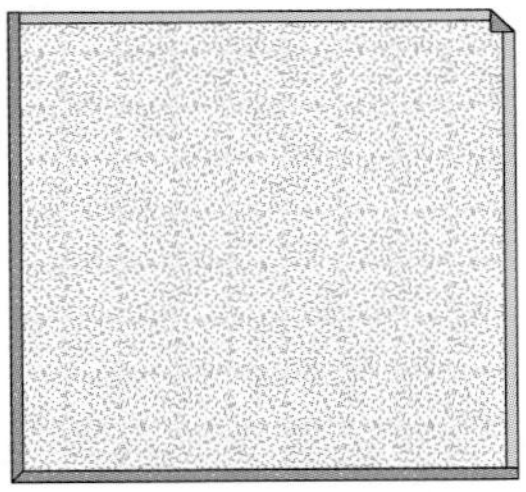

Fig 23

15. Blind stitch binding to backing, folding raw edges under 1/4" as you sew.

Strawberries & Cream

by Nancy Brenan Daniel
Tempe, Arizona

APPROXIMATE SIZE: 20" X 24"

Nancy has used her artistic ability and innovative mind to create picture-perfect Log Cabin blocks that become a field of strawberries for Sue. Known for her time-saving techniques Nancy is the author of a number of books published by ASN.

The setting for this little Sunbonnet Sue holding a cream pitcher is pieced by using a variety of rapid and traditional techniques, demonstrating that the techniques are compatible and even complement each other. The quilt answers one of the questions Nancy is often asked, "Are you a rapid or a traditional piecer?" Nancy's answer, "I'm both!"

Fabric Requirements:
1/3 yd muslin (background)
1/4 yd red (Strawberry Block and Shoe)
1/4 yd pink (Heart Block)
1/4 yd med blue print (star points)
1/4 yd dk blue print (border, binding, Bonnet)
assorted scraps (Apron, Dress, Sleeve, Hand, Pitcher and Leaves)
2/3 yd backing
28" x 32" batting

Additional Supplies:
embroidery floss (green for stems and gold for pitcher)
freezer paper

Pattern Pieces (pages 73 and 78):
7" Sunbonnet Sue
Pitcher
Leaf

Shown in full color on page 11.

Cutting Requirements:
two 1 1/4" x 18" strips, red
one 1 1/4" x 18" strip, muslin
four 1 1/4" x 31" strips, pink
one 1 1/4" x 31" strip, muslin
fourteen 2" x 2" squares, med blue (cut diagonally in half to form 28 triangles)
62 - 2" squares, muslin (cut diagonally in half to form 124 triangles)
52 - 1 5/8" x 1 5/8" squares, med blue
29 - 2 5/8" squares, muslin
three 2 5/8"-wide strips, dk blue print (border)
three 2" x 42" strips, dk blue print (binding)

Instructions:

Strawberry and Heart Blocks

STRAWBERRIES
1. Place 1 1/4" x 18" red and muslin strips right sides together; sew along length, **Fig 1**. Press seam allowance toward darker fabric.

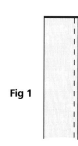

Fig 1

2. Cut strips into 1 1/4" units, **Fig 2**.

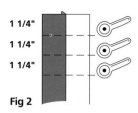

Fig 2

3. Place unit right sides together with remaining red strip; stitch. Continue adding and sewing red/muslin units along red strip, **Fig 3**. Be sure that muslin square is **always** at top.

Fig 3

4. Cut units apart, **Fig 4**, and press seam toward red strip. You will have fourteen strawberries, **Fig 5**.

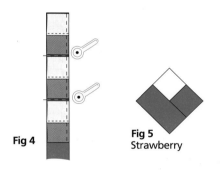

Fig 4

Fig 5
Strawberry

HEARTS
Repeat steps 1 to 4 above using 1 1/4" x 31" pink and muslin strips. You will need 24 hearts, **Fig 6**.

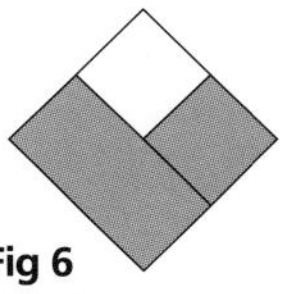

Fig 6
Heart

FINISHING THE BLOCKS

1. Sew 2" muslin triangles to opposite sides of a heart; sew 2" muslin triangle to remaining sides, **Fig 7**. Make a total of ten blocks.

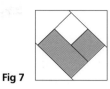

Fig 7

2. Sew a 2" med blue triangle to one side of a heart and a 2" muslin triangle to the opposite side; repeat on remaining two sides, **Fig 8**. Make a total of 14 blocks.

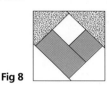

Fig 8

3. Sew a 2" muslin triangle to opposite sides of a strawberry; repeat on remaining sides, **Fig 9**. Make a total of 14 blocks.

Fig 9

4. Trim Heart and Strawberry Blocks to 2 5/8" square. You should have a 1/4" seam allowance from each point of the strawberry or heart to edge of block.

Star Points

1. Place a 1 5/8" med blue square right sides together at one corner of a 2 5/8" muslin square; stitch from corner to corner, **Fig 10**.

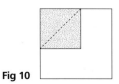

Fig 10

2. Snip excess corner leaving a 1/4" seam allowance, **Fig 11**.

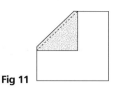

Fig 11

3. Flip triangle over seam allowance and press in place, **Fig 12**.

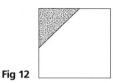

Fig 12

4. Repeat steps 1 to 3 at opposite corner, then remaining two corners, **Fig 13**.

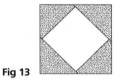

Fig 13

5. Repeat steps 1 to 4 for a total of ten blocks.

6. Repeat steps 1 to 3 at two adjacent corners for a total of six blocks, **Fig 14**.

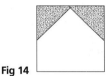

Fig 14

Assembling the Quilt

1. Referring to layout (page 26), place Strawberry Blocks, Heart Blocks, Star Points and plain squares in rows. Sew together in rows, then sew rows together.

2. Measure the length of the quilt; cut two 2 5/8"-wide dk blue print strips to that length. Sew to each side of quilt.

3. Measure the width of the quilt; cut two 2 5/8"-wide dk blue print strips to that length. Sew a Strawberry Block to each end of each strip; sew to top and bottom of quilt.

continued

Appliqué and Embroidery

1. Using two strands of green embroidery floss, Chain Stitch a stem on each strawberry, **Fig 15**.

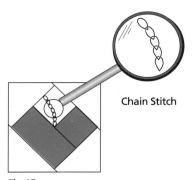

Chain Stitch

Fig 15

2. Trace and cut 14 Leaves, one Pitcher, one Bonnet, one Dress, one Apron, one Sleeve, one Hand, and one Shoe from freezer paper. Cut each piece from appropriate fabric, cutting 1/8"-1/4" from edge of freezer paper pattern.

3. Appliqué is done using Freezer Paper Method on page 5. Appliqué one leaf to each strawberry, **Fig 16**.

Fig 16

4. Appliqué Sunbonnet Sue in order: Shoe, Dress, Apron, Sleeve with Hand underneath, and Bonnet. Appliqué Pitcher, leaving room for handle.

5. Chain Stitch (see **Fig 15**) two rows for Pitcher handle using gold floss.

Finishing the Quilt

1. Place backing wrong side up, then batting and quilt top right side up. Baste by hand or with safety pins. Quilt as desired. Photographed quilt was machine quilted in the ditch, then hand quilted 1/4" from seam lines. Trim backing and batting even with quilt top.

2. Sew the 2" x 42" dk blue bias strips end to end to form one long strip. Fold in half lengthwise with wrong sides together; press.

3. Place binding strip along edge of back of quilt with raw edges even; stitch. Trim excess length of binding flush with top and bottom of quilt. Fold binding toward front of quilt over seam allowance; pin folded edge over seam, **Fig 17**. Finish top of binding by hand with blind stitch or by machine using a nylon thread and a very small zigzag stitch on folded edge of binding, **Fig 18**. Repeat on opposite side of quilt.

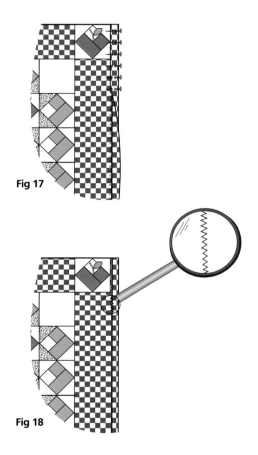

Fig 17

Fig 18

4. Repeat step 3 at top and bottom of quilt, except leave a 1/4" overlap at each end. Tuck ends under when sewing for a nice finish.

5. Stitch binding ends closed at corners by hand with matching thread.

Sunbonnet Sue has a Picket Fence

by Bettina Havig
Columbia, Missouri

APPROXIMATE SIZE: 42" X 50"

A quilter, teacher, lecturer and quilt historian, Bettina began quilting in 1970 and has been teaching since 1974. She has taught classes ranging across the quilt spectrum. She has been on the faculty of a number of symposia and conferences, and her work has appeared in invitational shows. Last year she edited the first in the Quilt Guild Series for ASN Publishing.

Bettina's Sue and Sam stand primly behind their picket fences. When they are ready to leave the garden, they can exit through the gate at the end of the rows.

Fabric Requirements:
1/8 yd each of four green prints (trees)
1/2 yd blue sky (tree background)
1 3/4 yds sunflower floral (picket fence background, outer border and binding)
1/8 yd brown or tan (tree trunks)
1/4 yd black print (inner border)
3/4 yd white or white-on-white (picket fence)
1 yd (Sunbonnet Sue and Overall Sam background)
assorted scraps for appliqué (no more than 1/8 yd of any): small prints for Dresses and Aprons, black (Sue's) Shoes, straw-colored print for Bonnet, tiny print for Shirt, chambray or denim blue for Overalls, yellow-gold for Hat, brown (Sam's) Shoes and flesh for Hands
50" x 58" batting

Pattern Pieces (pages 72 and 81):
5" Sunbonnet Sue and Overall Sam
A Tree Triangle
B, B Reversed Background Triangle

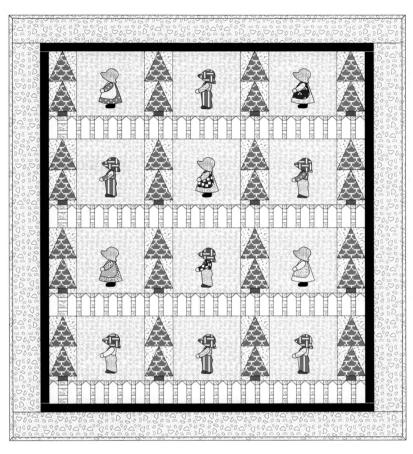

Shown in full color on page 10.

Cutting Requirements:
Note: *All strips are cut across the grain from selvage to selvage. Choose your faborite method of appliqué, pages 4 to 7, before cutting Sunbonnet Sue and Overall Sam's pattern pieces from fabric.*

six 5" Sunbonnet Sue, assorted fabrics
six 5" Overall Sam patterns, assorted fabrics
twelve 8" x 8" squares, lt tan (background for Sunbonnet Sue and Overall Sam)
eight 1 1/2"-wide strips cut into 92 - 1 1/2" x 3 1/2" pieces, white (pickets)
five 1"-wide strips cut into 184 - 1" squares, floral (picket background)
four 1 1/2"-wide strips, floral (fence connectors)
eight 1"-wide strips, floral (fence connectors)

eight 1"-wide strips, white (fence connectors)
two 1" x 6" strips, floral (gate connector)
one 1 1/2" x 6" strips, floral (gate connector)
two 1" x 6" strips, white (gate connector)
32 A Tree Triangles, assorted greens
32 B Background Triangles and 32 B Triangles reversed, blue (background for trees)
two 1 1/2"-wide strips, blue (tree trunk background)
one 1 1/2"-wide strip, brown (tree trunk)
five 1 1/4"-wide strips, black print (inner border)
five 3 1/2"-wide strips, floral (outer border)

continued

Making the Picket Fence

1. To make pickets, place a 1" floral square at corner of 1 1/2" x 3 1/2" white strip with right sides together; sew across square diagonally from edge to edge, **Fig 1**.

2. Trim seam allowance to 1/4", **Fig 2**; press open, **Fig 3**. Repeat with second floral square at adjacent corner, **Fig 4**. Make 92 pickets.

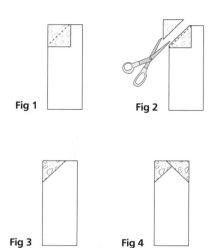

Fig 1   Fig 2

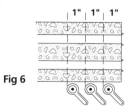

Fig 3   Fig 4

3. For fence connectors, sew strips together in this order: 1"-wide floral, 1"-wide white, 1 1/2"-wide floral, 1"-wide white and 1"-wide floral, **Fig 5**. Press seam allowances toward floral print. Repeat three times for a total of four strip groups.

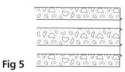

Fig 5

4. Cut strips into 1" units for a total of 84 fence connectors, **Fig 6**.

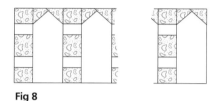

Fig 6

5. For the gate, sew the following strips together in same order as for fence connectors: 1" x 6" floral, 1" x 6"

white, 1 1/2" x 6" floral, 1" x 6" white, and 1" x 6" floral. Press seams toward floral fabric. Cut strips every 1 1/2" for a total of four gate connector pieces. Sew a picket to each side of a 1 1/2"-wide gate connector piece, **Fig 7**; Repeat for a total of four gates.

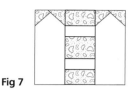

Fig 7

6. For fence row, alternate and sew 21 fence connectors and 21 pickets beginning with a fence connector and ending with a picket, **Fig 8**.

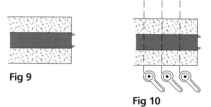

Fig 8

7. Sew gate to left end of fence to complete row. Repeat steps 6 and 7 for a total of four fence rows.

Making the Tree Blocks

1. For tree trunks, sew a 1 1/2"-wide blue strip to each side of a 1 1/2"-wide brown strip along length, **Fig 9**. Press seam allowances toward brown fabric. Cut strips into sixteen 1"-wide pieces, **Fig 10**.

Fig 9   Fig 10

2. For trees, sew blue B Background Triangle and blue B Background Triangle reversed to diagonal sides of green A Tree Triangle; press, **Fig 11**.

Fig 11

3. Sew a tree trunk to bottom of 16 trees, **Fig 12**. Sew tree to top edge of tree with trunk, **Fig 13**. Repeat for a total of 16 Tree Blocks.

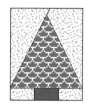

Fig 12

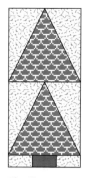

Fig 13

Making the Sunbonnet Sue and Overall Sam Blocks

1. Referring to Appliqué Techniques, pages 4 to 7, appliqué Sunbonnet Sue to each of six 8" x 8" lt tan squares.

2. Appliqué Overall Sam to each of six 8" x 8" lt tan squares.

Assembling the Quilt

1. Place Tree Blocks, Sunbonnet Sue Blocks, Overall Sam Blocks and Picket Fence rows according to layout on page 29.

2. Sew Tree Blocks and Sue and Sam Blocks in rows, then sew to fence rows.

3. Measure length of quilt; cut 1 1/4"-wide black print strips to that length. Sew to each side of quilt.

4. Measure width of quilt (including borders); cut 1 1/4"-wide black print strips to that length. Sew to top and bottom of quilt. Repeat for outer floral border using 3 1/2"-wide floral strips. Piece strips as necessary to achieve length needed.

5. Place backing wrong side up, then batting and quilt top right side up; baste by hand or with safety pins. Quilt as desired. Photographed quilt was hand quilted around each Sue and Sam and 1/4" from seam lines of Sue and Sam Blocks, pickets and trees.

6. Bind quilt referring to Attaching the Binding, page 8.

Sunbonnets' Shoes

by Dori Hawks
Salem, South Carolina

APPROXIMATE SIZE: 42" X 42"

Dori's trademark is her wearing of brightly-colored sneakers, so it is natural that Dori would put Sue in a setting of fun feet. Dori chose to use hand-dyed fabric for much of her quilt. Naturally, other fabric can be substituted. Dori couldn't stand the thought of covering up the beautiful hand-dyed fabrics she has been collecting so she used see-through netting for Sue's Apron.

Fabric Requirements:
one 6" square each of nine different
  hand-dyed fabrics (Dresses)
one 4" square each of 9 different
  hand-dyed fabrics (Bonnets)
one 6" square each of 9 different
  hand-dyed fabrics (Sleeves and
  Shoes)
one 8" square of pink hand-dyed
  fabric (Hands)
1/4 yd lime green tulle (Aprons)
5/8 yd lt large-scale print
  (background)
1/4 yd each of 8 to 10 different
  hand-dyed fabrics (Setting
  Triangles)
1 1/4 yds hand-dyed fabric (border
  and binding)
3 1/2 yds (backing)
50" square lightweight batting

Additional Supplies:
one to two packages of tear away
  stabilizer
5 to 6 yds decorative metallic yarn
  or heavy thread
monofilament thread

Pattern Pieces (pages 73 and 78):
7" Sunbonnet Sue
Setting Triangle
Border Shoe

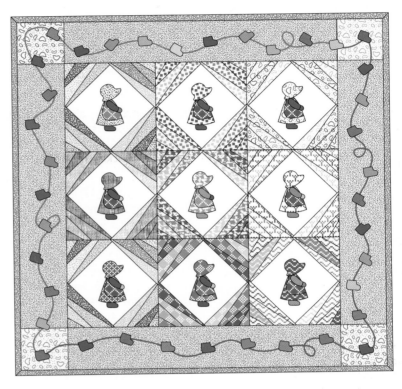

Shown in full color on page 11.

Cutting Requirements:
nine 8" squares, lt large-scale print
three 2 1/2"-wide (crosswise) strips,
  each of 8 to 10 different hand-dyed
  fabrics
four 5 1/2" x 25" strips, hand-dyed
  border fabric
four 5 1/2" squares, assorted
  hand-dyed fabrics
four 2 1/2" (crosswise) strips,
  hand-dyed border fabric

Instructions:

Read Appliqué Techniques, pages 4 to 7, to choose your favorite method of appliqué. Photographed model was appliquéd following Freezer Paper with School Paste, page 5.

Making the Quilt Top
1. Prepare all Sunbonnet Sue pieces except Apron for appliqué. You will need nine sets of 7" Sunbonnet Sue pattern pieces and 38 Border Shoes.

2. Cut out nine Aprons from tulle, adding 1/4" seam allowance to front and neck edges only, **Fig 1**. Place Apron on right side of Dress and fold seam allowance of Apron under front edge of Dress, **Fig 2**; pin in place. Repeat for all Aprons and Dresses.

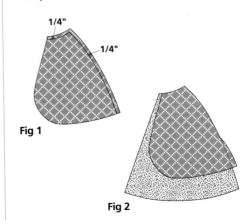

1/4"

1/4"

Fig 1

Fig 2

3. Place prepared Sunbonnet Sue pieces in center of 8" background square, **Fig 3**; pin in place.

Fig 3

4. Appliqué as desired. Photographed model was appliquéd by machine using a blind hem stitch and clear monofilament thread.

5. Trace 36 Setting Triangles onto paper; cut out leaving a 1/4" seam allowance along outside edges. Place two different 2 1/2"-wide strips right sides together on unmarked side of paper foundation, overlapping first (longest) line by 1/4", **Fig 4**. Turn paper over and sew on marked line. *Hint: Use a very short stitch length so it will be easier to tear paper away later.*

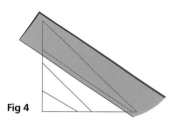

Fig 4

6. Fold top strip open and finger press; trim excess fabric. Place third strip right sides together with second strip; turn over and sew on marked line. Trim seam allowance to 1/4". Fold over, finger press, and trim excess strip. Repeat with fourth strip. Trim fabric even with paper foundation. Repeat for a total of 36 Setting Triangles, **Fig 5**, using the same fabrics for each block's set of four Setting Triangles.

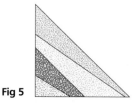

Fig 5

Hint: Do not tear the paper away until you have the quilt pieced and the border attached as the edges will be somewhat on the bias and could stretch.

7. Sew two Setting Triangles to opposite sides of a Sunbonnet Sue Block; sew two Setting Triangles to remaining sides, **Fig 6**. Repeat for all nine Sunbonnet Sue Blocks.

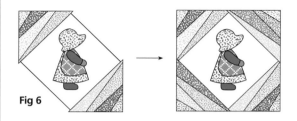

Fig 6

Finishing the Quilt

1. Sew blocks together in three rows of three blocks; sew rows together.

2. Measure length and width of quilt top. Cut 5 1/2"-wide borders to that length. Sew a border strip to opposite sides of quilt top. Sew a 5 1/2" square to each end of each remaining border strip; sew to top and bottom of quilt top.

3. Pin decorative metallic yarn in random curves and loops on border; refer to layout, page 31 and photograph, page 11 for placement idea. Place tear away stabilizer under border area, then using a long, narrow zigzag stitch and monofilament thread, sew metallic yarn in place. Remove tear away stabilizer.

4. Appliqué Border Shoes randomly along metallic thread.

5. Place backing wrong side up, then batting and quilt top right side up. Baste by hand or with safety pins.

6. Quilt as desired. Photographed quilt is machine quilted in the ditch between the blocks and the border using monofilament thread. The appliqué sections are quilted around each piece and along the couched thread.

7. Refer to Attaching the Binding, page 8, to attach binding.

The Stars of Today's Show

by Myrna Giesbrecht
Kamloops BC, Canada

APPROXIMATE SIZE: 48" X 48"

Sunbonnet Sue and Overall Sam are the shining stars in Myrna's beautifully quilted star setting for this sweet couple. Myrna, the author of four quilting books, is a master of time-saving techniques. That's so she has time to enjoy camping, reading, power walking, fabric shopping, doing lunch and talking on the phone.

Fabric Requirements:

2 1/2 yds off-white background fabric
3/4 yd blue floral fabric
7/8 yd blue print fabric
5/8 yd binding fabric
2 7/8 yds backing fabric
scraps of fabrics for Sue and Sam
56" square, batting

Additional Supplies:

3/4 yd paper-backed fusible web

Pattern Pieces (pages 73, 76 and 78):

7" Sunbonnet Sue
7" Overall Sam
Heart

Cutting Requirements:

two 18" x 20" rectangles, background fabric
one 13" x 20" rectangle, background fabric
one 16 1/2" square, background fabric
two 5 1/4" squares, background fabric
eight 2 1/2" x 4 1/2" rectangles, background fabric
four 4 1/2" x 6 1/2" rectangles, background fabric
four 10 1/2" squares, background fabric
twelve 2 1/2" squares, background fabric
ten 2 1/2" x 45" strips, background fabric (borders)
one 13" x 20" rectangle, blue floral
6" x 45" strip, blue floral (Hearts)
two 18" x 20" rectangles, blue print
four 6 1/2" squares, blue print

Shown in full color on page 15.

two 5 1/4" squares, blue print
eight 2 1/2" x 4 1/2" rectangles, blue print
eight 2 1/2" squares, blue print
five 2 1/4"-wide strips, blue floral
eight Hearts, blue floral

Instructions:

Making Block A and Block B

1. Place 13" x 20" blue floral rectangle right sides together with 13" x 20" background rectangle. Beginning at least 1/2" from top and left edges, draw a grid of six squares across and four squares down on the wrong side of the lightest fabric; space lines 2 7/8" apart, **Fig 1**.

2. Draw a diagonal line through every other square alternating between rows, **Fig 2**.

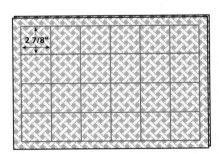

Fig 1

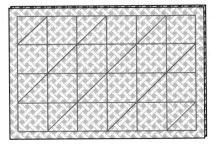

Fig 2

continued

3. Draw a diagonal line in the opposite direction through the remaining squares, **Fig 3**.

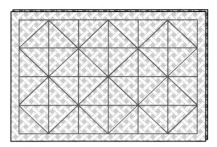

Fig 3

4. Stitch 1/4" away on both sides of the drawn lines, **Fig 4**; press to set stitches.

Fig 4

5. Cut apart on all drawn lines, **Fig 5**.

Fig 5

6. Repeat for the 18" x 20" blue print and background rectangles drawing a grid with six squares across and five squares down. You will need 112 half square triangles with background and blue print fabrics and 40 half square triangles with background and blue floral fabrics, **Fig 6**.

make 112 with blue print

Fig 6 make 40 with blue floral

7. Place blue print/background half square triangles, 2 1/2" background square, 2 1/2" blue print square, 2 1/2" x 4 1/2" background rectangle and 2 1/2" x 4 1/2" blue print rectangle as in **Fig 7**; sew together in rows, then sew rows together. Make four each of Blocks A and B.

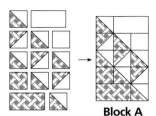

Fig 7 **Block A** **Block B**

Making Block C

1. Place a 5 1/4" background square right sides together with a 5 1/4" blue square matching corners, **Fig 8**; press.

Fig 8

2. Draw a diagonal line from corner to corner on wrong side of lightest fabric; stitch 1/4" from both sides of drawn line, **Fig 9**. Press to set stitches.

Fig 9

3. Cut apart on drawn line, **Fig 10**. Press open

Fig 10

4. Cut diagonally across each half square triangle creating two pieced halves, **Fig 11**. Redistribute and stitch together to form quarter square triangles, **Fig 12**.

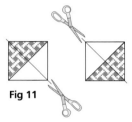

Fig 11

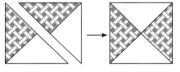

Fig 12

5. Stitch a quarter square triangle to a 4 1/2" x 6 1/2" background rectangles forming Block C, **Fig 13**.

6. Repeat steps 1 to 5 for a total of four Block C.

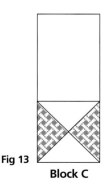

Fig 13

Block C

Sue and Sam Center Block

1. Press the four 6 1/2" blue print squares in half diagonally, wrong sides together.

2. Position a blue print square right sides together in corner of the 16 1/2" background square, **Fig 14**.

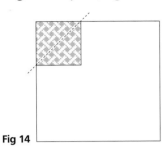

Fig 14

3. Stitch on the pressed diagonal line; trim away corner of blue print fabric only, leaving background square intact, **Fig 15**.

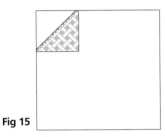

Fig 15

4. Fold the blue print corner back and press triangle in place. Repeat steps 2 to 4 at each corner to complete center block, **Fig 16**.

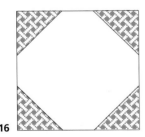

Fig 16

5. Prepare Sunbonnet Sue and Overall Sam pieces following Appliqué with Paper-backed Fusible Webbing, page 6. Remember to mirror Sam so that he'll be facing Sue. Remove paper backing

and position pieces in center of 16 1/2" background square, **Fig 17**.

Fig 17

6. Use a short, narrow zigzag stitch to secure raw edges around and within the figures.

Fig 19

Making the Star

1. Stitch one each of Blocks A, B, and C together, **Fig 18**. Make four. These form the star point sections.

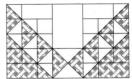

Fig 18

2. Place Blocks A, B, C, Sue and Sam Center Block and 10 1/2" background squares as in **Fig 19**. Sew together in rows, then sew rows together.

3. Trace Heart pattern onto paper backing of fusible web eight times. Separate and fuse to the 6" x 45" blue floral strip; trim. Remove paper backing and fuse in place. Follow Appliqué with Paper-backed Fusible Webbing and zigzag in place where shown in **Fig 20**.

Fig 20

continued

Borders

1. For first border, sew a 2 1/2"-wide background strip to top and bottom of quilt, then sew to each side. If an accurate 1/4" seam allowance has been stitched, the top and bottom borders will measure 2 1/2" x 36 1/2" and the side borders 2 1/2" x 40 1/2". Measure and fit borders to your quilt top specifically to ensure it lays flat and even around the edges.

2. For second border, sew ten blue print/background half square triangles and ten blue floral/background half square triangles alternately to form borders, **Fig 21**. Repeat for a total of four strips.

3. Sew a 2 1/2" background square to each end of two pieced border strips, **Fig 22**. These will be the side borders.

5. For third border, sew 2 1/2"-wide background strip to top and bottom, then to each side to complete quilt top.

Finishing the Quilt

1. Place backing wrong side up, then batting and quilt top right side up. Baste by hand or with safety pins. Quilt as desired. The photographed quilt has 1/2" cross hatching through the center square, stipple quilting in the outer points and stipple quilted hearts within the valleys created by the pieced border.

2. Refer to Attaching the Binding, page 8, to add binding.

Fig 21

Fig 22

4. Stitch pieced borders to the top and bottom and then the sides of the central design, **Fig 23**.

Fig 23

36

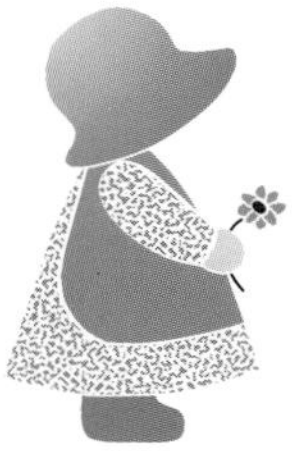

Lost in the Stars

by Meredith Montross
La Jolla, California

APPROXIMATE SIZE: 17 1/2" X 17 1/2"

Meredith's one-piece Sues are mere shadows in a starry sky. Not only did she create her Star Blocks from star fabric, but she has also quilted stars around the border of her little quilt. Meredith is able to enjoy her love of quilting every day because she works in the quilting department of ASN Publishing.

Fabric Requirements:

1/2 yd dk blue star print
1/2 yd off-white star print
1/4 yd yellow star print
22" square batting

Additional Supplies:

matching thread
gold metallic thread

Pattern Pieces (pages 72 and 88):

3" Sunbonnet Sue Shape
Star Quilting Pattern

Cutting Requirements:

eight 2 1/2" squares, dk blue star print
sixteen 1 1/2" squares, dk blue star print
one 8" x 12" rectangle, dk blue star print
one 8" x 16" rectangle, dk blue star print
one 8" x 12" rectangle, off-white star print
one 8" x 16" rectangle, yellow star print
two 1 1/4" x 12 1/2" strips, yellow star print (inner border)
two 1 1/4" x 13 1/2" strips, yellow star print (inner border)
four 2 1/2" x 13 1/2" strips, off-white star print (outer border)
four 2" x 18" strips, dk blue star print (binding)
four Sunbonnet Sue Shapes and four reversed, off-white star print - cut out after reading Appliqué with Lining fabric, page 6.

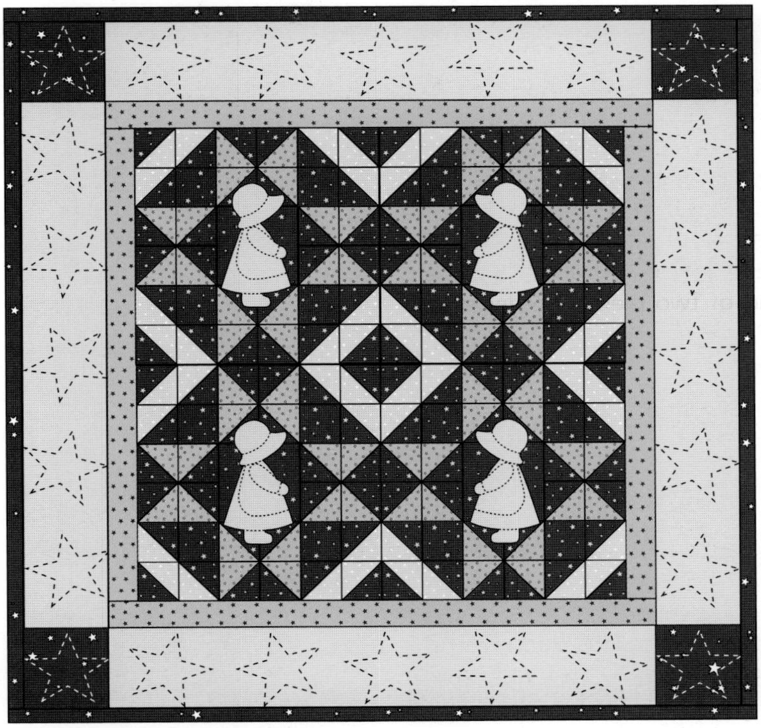

Shown in full color on page 11.

Instructions:

Making Triangle Squares

1. For dk blue/off-white triangle squares, draw 1 7/8" grid, four squares across and six squares down, on wrong side of an off-white 8" x 12" rectangle, **Fig 1**.

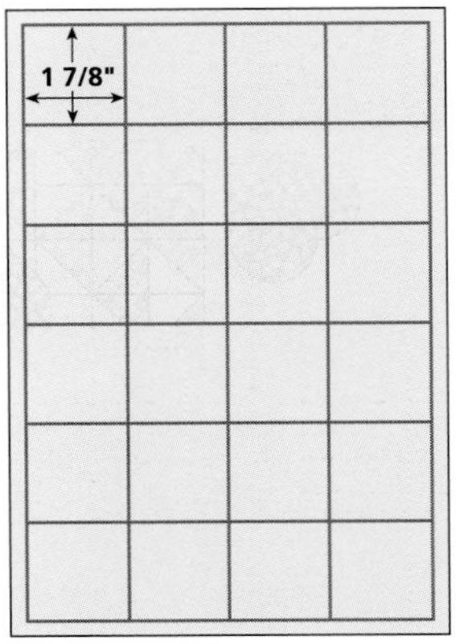

Fig 1

2. Draw diagonal line through every square, **Fig 2**.

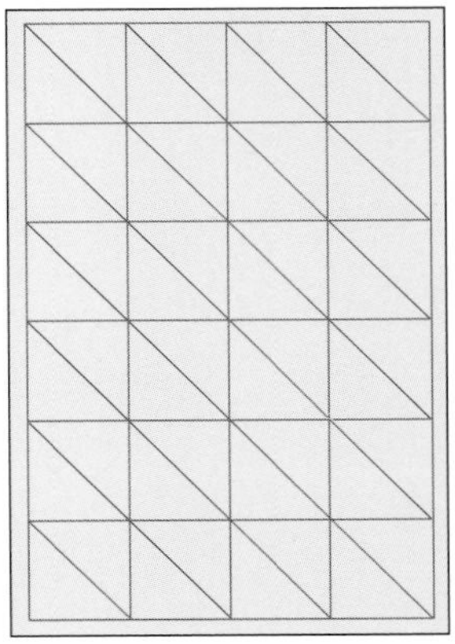

Fig 2

continued

3. Place marked rectangle right sides together with 8" x 12" dk blue rectangle; sew 1/4" from each side of marked diagonal lines, **Fig 3**.

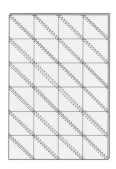

Fig 3

4. Cut along all drawn lines, **Fig 4**.

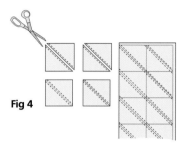

Fig 4

5. Press seams toward darker fabric; clip dog ears, **Fig 5**. You will have a total of 48 dk blue/off-white triangle squares.

Fig 5

6. Repeat steps 1 to 5 for dk blue/ yellow triangle squares using 8" x 16" dk blue star print and yellow star print rectangles. Draw 1 7/8" grid of four squares across and eight squares down, **Fig 6**. You will have a total of 64 blue/yellow triangle squares.

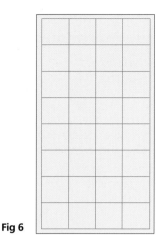

Fig 6

Star Blocks

1. For dk blue/off-white blocks, sew two dk blue/off-white triangle squares together, **Fig 7**.

Fig 7

2. Sew one dk blue/off-white triangle square to one 1 1/2" dk blue star print square, **Fig 8**.

Fig 8

3. Sew the two rows together, **Fig 9**.

Fig 9

4. Repeat steps 1 to 3 for a total of sixteen dk blue/off-white blocks.

5. For dk blue/yellow blocks, sew two dk blue/yellow triangle squares together, **Fig 10**; repeat for a total of 32 pairs.

Fig 10

6. Sew two pairs together, **Fig 11**; repeat for a total of sixteen dk blue/yellow blocks.

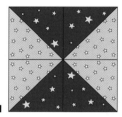

Fig 11

7. Arrange dk blue/off-white blocks, dk blue/yellow blocks and 2 1/2" dk blue square block as in **Fig 12**. Sew together in rows.

Fig 12

8. Press seams for first and third rows to the right and second row to the left for ease in sewing rows together, **Fig 13**. Sew rows together.

Fig 13

9. Repeat steps 7 and 8 for a total of four Star Blocks.

Sunbonnet Sue

Read Appliqué Techniques, pages 4 to 7, before beginning. Appliqué with Lining Fabric, page 6, was used for this quilt.

1. Cut out four Sunbonnet Sue Shapes from off-white star print; flop pattern and cut out four more for lining.

2. Appliqué Sue to center of each Star Block. Two Sunbonnet Sues will face left and two will face right.

3. Outline Sleeve, Apron, Shoe and Bonnet using a hand quilting (running) stitch and matching quilting thread, **Fig 14**.

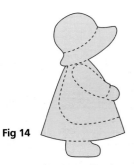

Fig 14

Finishing the Quilt

1. Sew the four Star Blocks together matching seams. *Hint: Place a pin at matching seams to hold in place for sewing.*

2. Sew yellow inner border to sides first, then top and bottom.

3. Sew 2 1/2"-wide off-white outer border to each side of quilt. Sew 2 1/2" dk blue square to each end of remaining two 2 1/2"- wide off-white strips; sew to top and bottom of quilt.

4. Place backing wrong side up, then batting and quilt top right side up. Baste by hand or with safety pins.

5. Quilt as desired. Photographed quilt was quilted around the Sunbonnet Sue Shapes and in-the-ditch around stars and inner border. Star quilting pattern (page 88) was quilted in off-white border using dk blue thread and in dk blue squares using gold metallic thread.

6. Add binding referring to Attaching the Binding, page 8.

Black Tie

by Kim DeCoste
Houston, Texas

APPROXIMATE SIZE: 29 1/2" X 36"

Naturally our one male quilter would choose to devote his quilt to Overall Sam. But his Overall Sam has just been dragged kicking and screaming into the 90s with a new look. Instead of Sam's usual country casual, he's now outfitted in a top hat and black tie.

Although the quilts in this collection were supposed to use the same pattern pieces, an exception was made in this case to give Sam his top hat. His black ties actually appear in the Bow Tie Blocks which surround Sam and the red buttons are the front of Sam's tuxedo. Said Kim, "It's been fun to collect black and white prints and great to have a chance to use so many of them."

Fabric Requirements:
3/4 yd white solid
1/8 yd of at least 6 different white prints (background)
1/8 yd of at least 6 different black prints
*3/8 yd black print (binding if cut on straight grain)
1/4 yd red or wine solid
1 yd backing fabric
38" x 44" batting
*Allow 1/2 yd for binding if cut on the bias.

Additional Supplies:
eighteen red buttons, 1/2" diameter

Pattern Pieces (pages 76, 79 and 80):
7" Overall Sam (except Hat)
A Small Square
B Background
C Large Square (4 1/2")
D Side Triangle
E Corner Triangle
F Border Strip
G Border Triangle
H Border Strip
I Border Strip
J Top Hat

Shown in full color on page 14.

Cutting Requirements:
*32 A Small Squares, assorted black prints
*64 B Backgrounds, assorted black prints (two per Bow Tie Block)
**64 B Backgrounds, assorted white prints (two per Bow Tie Block)
14 C Large Squares, white solid
18 D Side Triangles, white solid (watch grainline)
4 E Corner Triangles, white solid
one 8 1/2" x 8 1/2"square, white solid
five 1" x 44" strips, red solid
eight F Border Strips, assorted black prints
eight F Border Strips reversed, assorted black prints
two G Border Triangles, black prints
four H Border Strips, assorted black prints
four H Border Strips reversed, assorted black prints

two I Border Strips, assorted black prints

* Use one A Small Square and two B Backgrounds of the same black print per Bow Tie Block.

** Use two B Backgrounds of the same white print per Bow Tie Block.

Instructions:

Making the Bow Tie Block

1. Sew a black print B Background to opposite sides of black print A Square. Begin and end sewing 1/4" from each end, **Fig 1**.

Fig 1

40

2. Repeat step 1 with two white print B Backgrounds on remaining two sides of A Square, **Fig 2**.

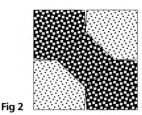

Fig 2

3. Sew corners, starting from inside corner and going towards outside edge, **Fig 3**. Repeat steps 1 to 3 for a total of 32 Bow Tie Blocks.

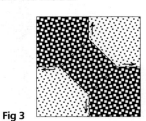

Fig 3

Making the Overall Sam Block

1. Fold 8 1/2" white background square in half diagonally; finger press. This gives a vertical placement for Sam.

2. Prepare appliqué pieces using your favorite method of appliqué in Appliqué Techniques, pages 4 to 7. Center the appliqué pieces on the 8 1/2" square; appliqué in place using a blind stitch.

Finishing the Quilt

1. Fold the 1"-wide red strips in half lengthwise with wrong sides together; press to create strips 1/2" wide.

2. Cut one folded red strip into four 8 1/2" lengths. Align cut edge of strip with cut edge of center square; pin in place. Repeat on all four sides of center appliqué, **Fig 4**.

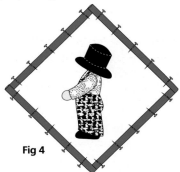

Fig 4

3. Refer to quilt layout (page 40) and place Bow Tie blocks and solid filler squares around Overall Sam Block. Continue adjusting Bow Tie Blocks until you have a pleasing and balanced composition.

4. Sew blocks together in diagonal rows, **Fig 5**, then sew rows together.

Fig 5

5. Pin four folded red strips to outer edge of pieced top (without border pieces) with raw edges even, **Fig 6**.

Fig 6

6. Piece side Border Strips H, F, F, I, F reversed, F reversed and H reversed referring to **Fig 7**. Attach to sides of quilt, sewing through all layers (red strips will form a 1/4" strip between blocks and border); begin and end stitching 1/4" from each end.

7. Piece top and bottom Border Strips H reversed, F reversed, F reversed, G, F, F and H referring to **Fig 8**. Attach to

top and bottom, sewing through all layers; begin and end stitching 1/4" from each end.

8. Sew border at corners, sewing from inner corner toward outer edge, **Fig 9**; press top.

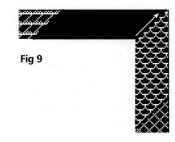

Fig 9

9. Layer backing wrong side up, then batting and quilt top right side up. Baste by hand or with safety pins.

10. Quilt as desired. Photographed quilt was hand quilted around bow ties and Overall Sam. Straight line quilting was done in the white squares.

11. Bind using 2 1/2"-wide binding referring to Attaching the Binding, page 8.

12. Referring to layout, page 40, and color photograph, page 13, sew three red buttons in each of six solid filler squares.

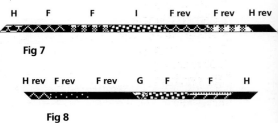

H   F   F   I   F rev   F rev   H rev

Fig 7

H rev F rev F rev G F   F   H

Fig 8

Sunbonnet Sue, Calendar Girl

by Marti Michell
Atlanta, Georgia

APPROXIMATE SIZE: 35" X 47"

One of the pioneers in the current quilt revival, Marti and her husband, Dick, owned a leading quilting supply company for 14 years. Today, she develops new products, designs fabrics, writes, teaches and consults on a freelance basis. Among the many books she has written, her **Quilting for People Who Don't Have Time to Quilt** *and* **Weekend Log Cabin Quilts**, *published by ASN Publishing have sold over a million copies.*

This wall hanging is a cross between playing with paper dolls and quilting. It is the perfect way to use some of the wonderful motif fabrics you have collected. Let the fabrics that you have collected do the work of representing the seasons, pastimes and fun of Sunbonnet Sue and Overall Sam. Because our challenge was to create projects with a minimum of extra pattern pieces, this was not only fun, but practical. It is especially fun if you have a design board and can rough cut and pin up samples and ideas without being in too much of a rush to complete. That allows you to look through your fabric for the bumble bee you didn't spot the first time, or didn't need until you put the sunflowers on Sue's Bonnet, etc. Even though Marti owned most of the fabrics represented when she started this quilt, she also admitted to buying a few more that made a better statement or were a better scale after she started the quilt.

Shown in full color on back cover.

Fabric Requirements:
assorted fabrics with "fun" themes
  and motifs
fat quarters (18" x 22 1/2") or fat
  eighths of 12 different black and
  white prints (backgrounds)
1/4 yd colorful stripe (first border)
1 yd bright print (second border and
  binding)
3/8 yd black print (sashing)
1 3/8 yds fabric (backing)
1/8 yd yellow solid (corner squares)
batting

Additional Supplies:
2 yds paper-backed fusible web
glue stick (optional)
assorted threads for Blanket
  Stitch trim

Pattern Pieces (pages 72, 74 and 77):
Alternate 7" Sunbonnet Sue
Alternate 7" Overall Sam
3" Sunbonnet Sue

Cutting Requirements:
eight 6 1/2" x 9 1/2" rectangles,
  assorted black and white prints
  (background)
four 13 1/2" x 9 1/2" rectangles,
assorted black and white prints
(background)
two 1 1/2" x 27 1/2" strips, black print
  (top and bottom sashing strips)

twelve 1 1/2" x 6 1/2" strips, black print
  (horizontal sashing strips)
eight 1 1/2" x 9 1/2" strips, black print
  (vertical sashing strips)
nine 1 1/2" squares, bright prints
  (sashing squares)
two 1 1/2" x 39 1/2" strips, colorful
  stripe (first border)
two 1 1/2" x 27 1/2" strips, colorful
  stripe (first border)
two 3 1/4" x 29 1/2" strips, bright print
  (second border)
two 3 1/4" x 41 1/2" strips, bright print
  (second border)
four 3 1/4" squares, yellow solid
  (corner squares)
five 2 1/2"-wide strips, bright print
  (binding)

Instructions:

Picking the Themes

The months represented in this quilt go across the rows: January is for Sewing; February is Valentine's Day; March is for St. Patrick; April is showers, flowers and Easter; May is Mother's Day; June is in the Garden; July is for picnics; August is Sunflowers and playing; September is back to school; October is Halloween; November is harvest and Thanksgiving; and December is Christmas. There are lots of other options that you could use to personalize your calendar such as a June wedding or personal wedding anniversary month, other religious holidays, a more patriotic 4th of July or other National holidays, sporting events, family reunion months, and personal favorite pastimes for which you have appropriate printed fabric.

Piecing the Blocks

1. Decide which background fabric you will use for a particular month and place according to layout. Notice that there are two smaller rectangles and one larger rectangle in each row.

2. Sew background rectangles together in rows with sashing strips in between, **Fig 1**; press seams in one direction. Sew rows together with sashing strips between; press.

Fig 1

Appliquéing the Blocks

1. Using the Appliqué with Paper-backed Fusible Web technique, page 6, prepare twelve of each 7" Alternate Sunbonnet Sue pattern piece, four of each 7" Alternate Overall Sam pattern piece and two of each 3" Sunbonnet Sue pattern piece.

2. Draw patterns on paper side of the paper-backed fusible web. Note that four Sunbonnet Sue figures face to the right and eight face to the left. Two Overall Sam figures face left and two face right. Remember that the figures will face the opposite direction that is drawn on the fusible web.

3. Following manufacturer's directions, fuse all shapes to wrong side of appropriate fabric. Cut out along drawn lines.

4. Fuse paper-backed web to wrong side of selected fabric motifs.

5. Referring to **Fig 2** and photograph on back cover for placement ideas, arrange Sunbonnet Sue and Overall Sam shapes on background rectangles, starting with shoes about 1/2" from bottom edge. Note that the two 3"

Sunbonnet Sue figures are in the May block and overlap into the sashing. Position assorted theme motifs as desired on and around Sue and Sam. Let some of the motifs overlap some of the sashing strips.

6. When you are comfortable with the look of the blocks, begin to fuse the pieces. Remove the protective paper from the backs of the pieces and fuse them in place, working from the bottom up. You may want to stitch around the outside edge of the dress with contrasting quilting or decorative machine stitching thread before fusing the Sleeve or Bonnet in place.

Finishing the Quilt

1. Sew first border to sides of quilt first, then to top and bottom

2. Sew second border to sides first. Sew yellow corner square to each end of remaining border strips; sew to top and bottom.

3. Layer backing wrong side up, then batting and quilt top right side up. Baste by hand or with safety pins.

4. Quilt as desired.

5. Refer to Attaching the Binding, page 8, to add binding.

Fig 2

Sunbonnet Sue's Alive & Well
at The American School of Needlework®

by Bobbie Matela
Encinitas, California

APPROXIMATE SIZE: 22 1/2" X 27 3/4"

After ten years of editing quilt manuscripts in her position as Vice President and Managing Editor of the American School of Needlework® (ASN Publishing), Bobbie has finally finished a quilt. She was inspired by the chance to have a quilt published in a book she produced and got it finished (as usual) because of a deadline. The Schoolhouse and Spool Blocks represent the American School of Needlework, while Bobbie's three Sue appliqués are a tribute to the quilting, crochet and cross stitch creators who contribute to the over 300 books in the ASN line.

Fabric Requirements:
one fat quarter each of seven prints (Sue Blocks, Schoolhouse background and first border)
assorted print and solid scraps
one 6 1/2" square, each of three assorted lt prints (background for Sue Blocks)
1/8 yd purple print (sashing)
1/4 yd gold print (third border)
1/4 yd puple solid (binding)
30" x 35" batting

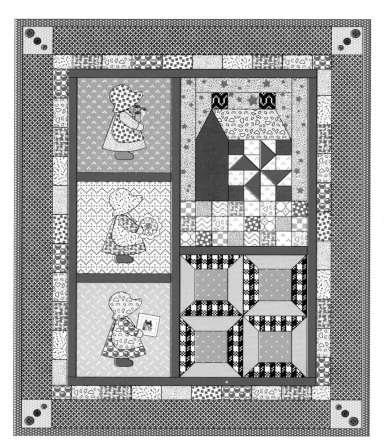

Shown in full color on page 12.

Additional Supplies:
Crocheted Doily or purchased doily motif
Size 20 off-white crochet cotton
Size 11 steel crochet hook
Cross Stitch House:
  2" square of 22-count Aida cloth
  Anchor Floss: rust 1014, gold 1002, purple 112 and lt yellow 292
  fabric sealant (such as Fray Check™)
four buttons, 3/8"
four buttons, 1/2"
four buttons, 3/4"
optional: brass letter charms (school house)

Pattern Pieces (pages 72 and 82):
5" Sunbonnet Sue
A Schoolhouse Front
B Schoolhouse Roof
C Schoohouse Corner
D Large Triangle
E Small Triangle
F Spool Side

Cutting Requirements:
Schoolhouse Block (make 1)
one A Schoolhouse Front, solid gold
one B Schoolhouse Roof, brown print
two 1 1/2" squares, rust print
one C Schoolhouse Corner, background fabric
one C Schoolhouse reversed, background fabric
one 1 1/2" x 2 1/2" rectangle, background fabric
one 1 1/2" x 6 1/2" strip, background fabric
two 1 1/2" x 8 1/2" strip, background fabric

eight 1 1/2" x 4 1/2" strips, four light and four dark fabrics
four 1 1/2" squares, solid gold
four D Large Triangles, purple print
eight E Small Triangles, yellow print
four 1 1/2" squares, yellow print
Sue Blocks (make 3)
three 6 1/2" squares, assorted small lt prints
three 2" x 2 1/2" rectangles, assorted prints (fabric rolls for quilter)
Spool Blocks (make 4)
eight F Spool Sides, dk fabric
eight F Spool Sides, lt fabric
four 2 1/2" squares, assorted colors
Pieced Rectangle
one 1 1/2" x 4 1/2" strip, each of four assorted lt prints and four assorted dk prints

44

Sashing

two 1 1/2" x 6 1/2" strips, purple print
one 1 1/2" x 8 1/2" strip, purple print
three 1 1/2" x 20 1/2" strips, purple print
two 1 1/2" x 17 1/2" strips, purple print

First Border

one 2 1/2" x 14" strip, each of six colors

Second Border

two 2 1/2" x 19 1/2" strips, gold print
two 2 1/2" x 24 1/2" strips, gold print
four 2 1/2" squares, lt solid (corner squares)

Binding

four 2"-wide strips, purple solid

Instructions:

Schoolhouse Block

1. Sew an E Small Triangle to both diagonal edges of D Large Triangle, **Fig 1**. Repeat for a total of four triangle units.

Fig 1

2. Sew a 1 1/2" gold square to a 1 1/2" yellow print square, **Fig 2**. Repeat for a total of four pairs of squares.

Fig 2

3. Sew triangle unit to pair of squares to complete a sub-unit, **Fig 3**. Repeat three more times.

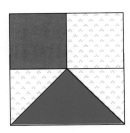

Fig 3

4. Sew four sub-units to complete Pinwheel Block for schoolhouse side, **Fig 4**.

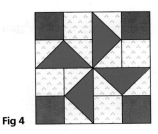

Fig 4

5. Sew B Schoolhouse Roof to top edge of Pinwheel Block, **Fig 5**.

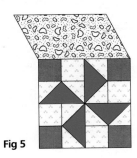

Fig 5

6. Sew A Schoolhouse Front to side and roof; sew from inside corner toward outside edge, **Fig 6**.

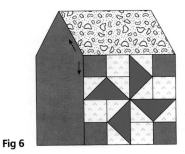

Fig 6

7. Sew 1 1/2" rust print square to opposite ends of 1 1/2" x 2 1/2" background strip. Sew to top of roof, **Fig 7**; start and stop stitching 1/4" from edge.

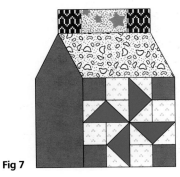

Fig 7

8. Sew C Schoolhouse Corner to schoolhouse front and chimney, sewing from inside corner to outside edges, **Fig 8**. Repeat for C Schoolhouse reversed piece.

Fig 8

9. Sew 1 1/2" x 6 1/2" background strip to top edge of Schoolhouse; sew 1 1/2" x 8 1/2" background strips to each side to complete Schoolhouse Block, **Fig 9**.

Fig 9

Spool Block

1. Sew a dk print F Spool Side to opposite sides of 2 1/2" square, **Fig 10**; start and stop stitching 1/4" from edge.

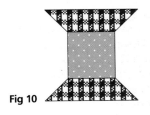

Fig 10

continued

2. Sew lt solid F Spool Side to remaining sides of square, **Fig 11**; start and stop stitching 1/4" from edge.

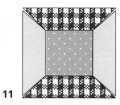

Fig 11

3. Sew diagonal seam, sewing from inner corner to outside edge, **Fig 12**.

Fig 12

4. Repeat steps 1 to 3 for three more spools.

5. Sew spools together to complete Spool Block, **Fig 13**.

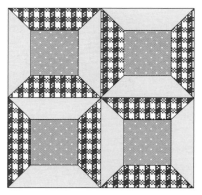

Fig 13

Pieced Rectangle

1. Sew a 1 1/2" x 4 1/2" lt print strip to a 1 1/2" x 4 1/2" dk print strip; cut at 1 1/2" intervals for pairs of squares, **Fig 14**.

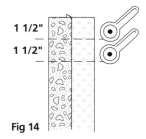

1 1/2"
1 1/2"

Fig 14

2. Repeat step 1 with three more pairs of strips; cut at 1 1/2" intervals for a total of 12 pairs of squares.

3. Sew four different pairs of squares end to end, **Fig 15**. Repeat for two more rows, placing pairs of squares in random order.

Fig 15

4. Press seams for rows 1 and 3 in one direction and row two in the opposite direction. Sew rows together to complete Pieced Rectangle, **Fig 16**.

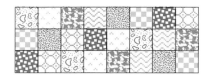

Fig 16

Sue Blocks

Note: One Sue is holding three rolls of quilting fabric, one is holding a small crochet doily and one is holding a small cross stitched piece. Refer to the color photograph on page 12, while making these three blocks.

CROCHETED DOILY

Size: About 1 3/4" diameter

Ch 4, join to form a ring.

Rnd 1: Ch 6 (counts as a dc and a ch-3 lp on this and following rnds), *dc in ring, ch 3; rep from * 6 times more; join in 3rd ch of beg ch-6: 8 ch-3 lps.

Rnd 2: Sl st in next ch3-lp; ch 1, in same lp work (sc, 3 dc, sc): petal made; in each rem ch-3 lp work (sc, 3 dc, sc): petal made; join in first sc: 8 petals.

Rnd 3: Sl st in next 2 dc; ch 1, sc in same dc as last sl st made; (ch 6, sc in 2nd dc of next petal) 7 times; ch 6; join in first sc.

Rnd 4: Sl st in next ch-6 lp; ch 1, in same lp work (sc, hdc, 5 dc, hdc, sc): petal made; in each rem ch-6 lp work (sc, hdc, 5 dc, hdc, sc): petal made; join in first sc.

Finish off and weave in ends.

CROSS STITCH SCHOOLHOUSE

1. Refer to the Schoolhouse Chart and stitch schoolhouse design onto Aida cloth using appropriate colors of floss. Use Cross Stitch, **Fig 17** and Running Stitch, **Fig 18**.

Schoolhouse Chart

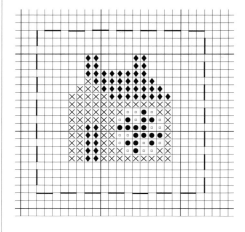

Color Key

▫ = yellow

✕ = gold

● = purple

◆ = rust

— = Running Stitch
  two strands purple

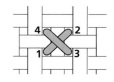

Fig 17 - Cross Stitch

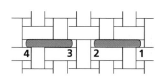

Fig 18 - Running Stitch

2. Cut Aida cloth about four squares from Running Stitch. Place fabric sealant along cut edges to prevent fraying.

FABRIC ROLLS

1. Fold the 2" sides of 2" x 2 1/2" fabric pieces toward center, **Fig 19**. Roll up entire length, **Fig 20**; tack in place.

2. Repeat for remaining two 2" x 2 1/2" fabric pieces.

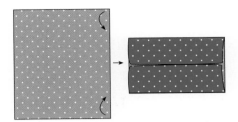

Fig 19

Fig 20

Appliquéing the Sue Blocks

1. Read Appliqué Techniques, pages 4 to 7, and prepare three Sunbonnet Sue figures for appliqué. The Spray Starch Method of Appliqué, page 5, was used in the photographed model.

2. Referring to Layout, page 44, place appliqué pieces centered on 6 1/2" background squares. Place crocheted doily under one Sue's hand, cross stitch design under the second and three rolls of fabric under the third. Pin all pieces in place.

3. Appliqué pieces to background using blind stitch.

4. Tack down doily, cross stitch design and fabric rolls.

Finishing the Quilt

1. Place blocks and sashing referring to layout, page 44.

2. Sew the three Sunbonnet Sue Blocks in a vertical row with 1 1/2" x 6 1/2" purple sashing strips between.

3. Sew Pieced Rectangle to lower edge of Schoolhouse Block; sew Spool Block to Pieced Rectangle with 1 1/2" x 8 1/2" purple sashing strip between.

4. Sew vertical rows of blocks alternating with 1 1/2" x 20 1/2" purple sashing strips; sew 1 1/2" x 17 1/2" sashing strip to top and bottom.

5. For first border, sew the six 2 1/2" x 14 1/2" strips together lengthwise; press seams in one direction. Cut at 1 1/2" intervals, **Fig 21**.

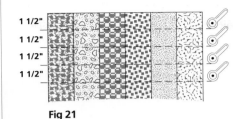

1 1/2"
1 1/2"
1 1/2"
1 1/2"

Fig 21

6. Sew two pieced strips together to form one long strip of twelve rectangles, **Fig 22**. Repeat for three more strips.

Fig 22

7. Remove one rectangle from each of two strips; sew to sides of quilt.

8. Mark center of top and bottom edge of quilt; mark center of remaining pieced borders. Trim equal amounts from each end of border strips to fit quilt, **Fig 23**. Sew border to top and bottom.

9. Sew 2 1/2"-wide gold print border to sides of quilt. Sew 2 1/2" lt solid square to each end of remaining two 2 1/2"-wide border strips; sew to top and bottom.

10. Layer quilt backing wrong side up, then batting and quilt top right side up. Baste by hand or with safety pins.

11. Quilt as desired. Photographed quilt was quilted in-the-ditch between blocks and sashing, between borders, around schoolhouse and around spools. A door was quilted in the Schoolhouse Front referring to pattern piece (page 82) for placement, diagonal lines in pieced rectangle, and diagonal lines in borders. Sunbonnet Sue's shape was echo quilted with lines spaced about 1/4" apart in the background square.

12. Refer to Attaching the Binding, page 8, to attach binding.

13. Sew three buttons in each corner square referring to photograph for placement.

14. Sew charms evenly spaced on Schoolhouse Front above door.

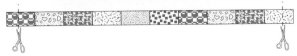

Fig 23

Sunbonnet Sweethearts

by Marti Michell
Atlanta, Georgia

APPROXIMATE SIZE: 17 1/4" X 22"

Another quilt by the creator of **Sunbonnet Sue, Calendar Girl**, *this wall hanging was inspired by a Norman Rockwell Saturday Evening Post cover.*

Marti affectionately calls her two sweethearts Bubba and Bubba Sue.

Fabric Requirements

assorted brown and pink fabric scraps (Sunbonnet Sue, Overall Sam and Hanging Hearts)
scrap, red/tan check (centers)
1/8 yd lt tan print
1/8 yd med tan floral
1/8 yd lt brown print
1/8 yd dk brown print
fat quarter (18" x 22"), pink print (Large Appliqué Heart)
fat quarter, brown plaid (border)
1/4 yd brown stripe (binding and dowel cover)
1/2 yd backing fabric
28" x 30" batting

Additional Supplies:

1/4 yd fusible non-woven interfacing
glue stick (optional)
small button for hat (optional)
9" length of 1/4"wide flat lace
1/2 yd 1/4"-wide off-white satin ribbon (Bonnet)
1 1/2 yds 1/16"-wide pink satin ribbon
1 yd 1/8"-wide off-white satin ribbon
1 yd 1/8"-wide tan satin ribbon
1 yd 1/4"-wide pink satin ribbon
1 yd 1/4"-wide brown satin ribbon
1 yd 1/4"-wide brown grosgrain ribbon
3/8" x 24" dowel (optional)
22" decorative Sunbonnet Sue quilt hanger (optional)
small amount of stuffing

Pattern Pieces (pages 74, 77, 83, and 84):

7" Alternate Sunbonnet Sue
7" Alternate Overall Sam
Large Appliqué Heart
Hanging Hearts 1, 2, 3, 4, 5 (optional)

Shown in full color on page 16.

Quilting Pattern (page 88):

Heart Border

Cutting Requirements:

four 1 1/2" x 2 1/2" strips, red/tan check
one of each of the following strips:
   1 1/2" x 11" strip, lt tan print (a)
   1 3/4" x 11" strip, lt tan print (b)
   1 1/2" x 21" strip, lt tan print (e)
   1 3/4" x 19" strip, lt tan print (f)
   1 1/2" x 30" strip, lt tan print (i)
   1 3/4" x 26" strip, lt tan print (j)
   1 3/8" x 16" strip, med tan floral (c)
   1 5/8" x 14" strip, med tan floral (d)
   1 3/8" x 25" strip, lt brown print (g)
   1 5/8" x 22" strip, lt brown print (h)
   1 5/8" x 35" strip, dk brown print (k)
   1 3/4" x 31" strip, dk brown print (l)
two 2 1/2" x 19" strips, brown plaid (border)

two 2 1/2" x 18 1/4" strips, brown plaid (border)
two 2 1/2"-wide strips, brown stripe (binding)
three 1 1/4" x 42" strips, brown stripe (dowel cover, optional)
one Large Appliqué Heart, pink print
four Hanging Hearts 1, assorted scraps
two Hanging Hearts 2, assorted scraps
two Hanging Hearts 3, assorted scraps
two Hanging Hearts 4, assorted scraps
one Hanging Heart 5, floral

Instructions:

About the Off-Center Log Cabin Block

Off-center Log Cabin blocks are made in the same manner as regular Log Cabin Blocks. However, both the off-centered and elongated design make the direction of the rotation much more crucial than in the typical block. Two of the blocks in this small wall hanging rotate clockwise and two counter clockwise.

The elongated design makes the light colored background space proportionate to body dimensions. The elongation is created by using a rectangle for the center instead of a square.

The off-center design creates both a pleasant background space and a nice framing for Overall Sam and Sunbonnet Sue. (If you are Southern, you may enjoy the same pet names we affectionately use, Bubba and Bubba Sue.) The off-center position is created by using different widths of strips on each side of the center rectangle.

Making the Off-Center Log Cabin Block

1. Place 1 1/2" x 2 1/2" red/tan check center strip right sides together with 1 1/2" x 11" lt tan strip (a); sew using a 1/4" seam allowance, **Fig 1**.

2. Without removing from sewing machine, place remaining red/tan check strips on lt tan strip and continue sewing until all four center strips are sewn, **Fig 2**.

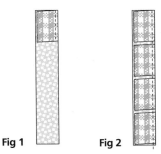

Fig 1   Fig 2

3. Cut lt tan strip even with center strips, **Fig 3**. Press toward darker fabric.

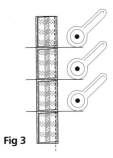

Fig 3

4. Turn center section so strip (a) is at top; place right sides together with 1 3/4" x 11" lt tan strip (b) and sew with 1/4" seam allowance, **Fig 4**; add another center and sew, **Fig 5**. Do not remove from sewing machine.

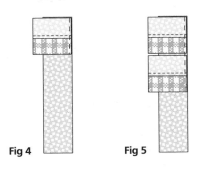

Fig 4   Fig 5

5. Turn another center section so strip (a) is at bottom; place right side down on same lt tan strip; sew. Add remaining center with strip (a) at bottom and sew, **Fig 6**.

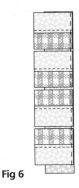

Fig 6

6. Trim lt tan strip even with center pieces, **Fig 7**.

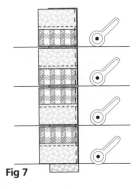

Fig 7

7. Continue adding strips until blocks are completed, making sure that two blocks are rotated clockwise and two are rotated counter clockwise, **Fig 8**. *Hint: After the first four strips are added (strip d), always add the next strip to the side that has three fabric pieces and two seams.*

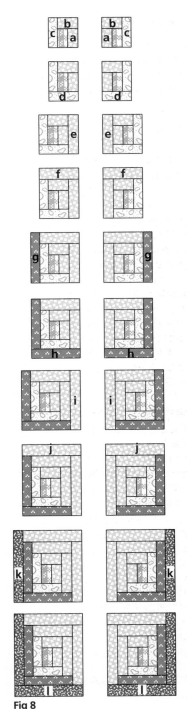

Fig 8

continued

Piecing the Quilt Top

1. Referring to **Fig 9**, place blocks together so dk brown strips are on the outside edge. Sew pairs of blocks, then sew pairs together.

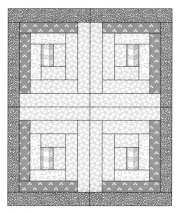

Fig 9

2. Sew dk brown plaid border to sides first, then to top and bottom.

Appliquéing Sunbonnet Sue and Overall Sam

The appliqué technique used could be called reinforced raw edge appliqué. That is, it isn't turned under and it isn't fused to the background. Instead, fusible non-woven interfacing is used to back the appliqué pieces and reinforce the raw edges of the fabric. The bonus is that the pieces have a softened look compared to straight fusing.

1. Trace Overall Sam pattern pieces on the non-fusible side of interfacing; trace Sunbonnet Sue pattern pieces in same manner, flopping all pattern pieces so that Sue will face Sam.

2. Fuse interfacing to wrong sides of all traced pieces; cut out along drawn line.

3. Trace, fuse and cut Large Appliqué Heart in same manner.

4. Position Large Appliqué Heart by having the dotted line (marked on pattern piece) match the horizontal seam of the four squares and the point match the vertical seam.

5. Referring to layout on page 48, position Sam and Sue on Heart; pin or glue (with glue stick) pieces in place. Place 1/4"-wide flat lace along edge of Apron; sew in place. Stitch around the outside edge with contrasting quilting or decorative machine stitching thread.

Photographed model was appliquéd by machine using the Blanket Stitch. It could also be done by hand, **Fig 10**.

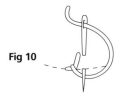

Fig 10

6. Tack 2" piece of 1/4"-wide ribbon to Bonnet above rim. Cut a 4" piece of ribbon; using remaining length of ribbon, make bow with two 3/4" loops on each side. Tie loops with 4" piece; trim all ends to desired length. Tack to Bonnet with heart button, **Fig 11**.

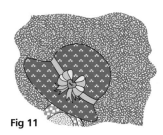

Fig 11

Assembling the Quilt

1. Place backing wrong side up, then batting and quilt top right side up. Baste by hand or with safety pins.

2. Quilt as desired. Photographed quilt was quilted following outline of Large Appliqué Heart in central portion of quilt.

The Heart Border pattern (page 88) was used for quilting in the dk brown border. Mark pattern from the corners of the border toward the center of each side. The extra loops in the center allow some flexibility in case the design doesn't fit perfectly. Just expand the loops to meet the hearts coming from the other corner.

3. If making covered dowel and loops, do not add binding at this time; continue with Making the Covered Dowel and Loops below. If not, refer to Attaching the Binding, page 8, to attach binding.

Making the Loops and Covered Dowel (optional)

If making the shirred dowel, make three fabric loops .

1. Cut three 5" x 5 1/2" rectangles from backing fabric. Fold in half right sides together across the 5" side; sew with 1/4" seam allowance, **Fig 12**.

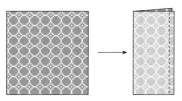

Fig 12

2. Turn right side out. Fold in half with seam inside and raw edges even. Tack evenly spaced to back of quilt, **Fig 13**.

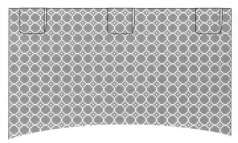

Fig 13

3. Refer to Attaching the Binding, page 8, to attach binding, making sure to catch loops when sewing binding to quilt top.

4. To make the shirred dowel, cut a fabric strip approximately four times as long and twice the diameter of the dowel plus 1/2 inch. For the 3/8" x 24" dowel used in photographed quilt, sew 1/14" x 42" strips together end to end; cut a 96" length.

5. Fold both ends toward the middle, but do not overlap. Sew along both long edges, **Fig 14**. Turn each half right side out from the center. Insert dowel and gather up until ends of dowel are at the end of the tube.

6. Place dowel through hanging loops.

fold  fold

Fig 14

Making Hanging Hearts

(optional)

Note: You can make as many or few of the stuffed hearts to hang from the dowel as desired.

1. Place two Heart 1 pieces right sides together; stitch leaving a small opening for turning, **Fig 15**. Repeat for another Heart 1, Heart 2 and Heart 3.

Fig 15

2. Turn hearts right side out through openings; add stuffing. Stitch openings closed.

3. Position a Heart 5 right side up on right side of Heart 4; appliqué in place using hand or machine Blanket Stitch, **Fig 16**. Place right sides together with another Heart 4; stitch, leaving opening for turning.

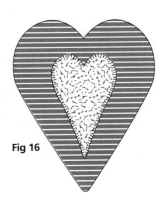

Fig 16

4. Tack Heart 4 and a Heart 1 on opposite ends of a 21" piece of brown grosgrain ribbon.

5. Make two 2" loops on one end of pink satin ribbon; tack Heart 3 to looped end, **Fig 17**.

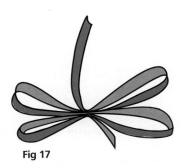

Fig 17

6. Tack a Heart 1 and Heart 2 to opposite ends of dk brown satin ribbon. Tack Heart 3 to one end of pink satin ribbon.

7. Tie all Hearts to dowel as desired.

8. Make small bows with remaining 1/16"-wide, 1/8"-wide and 1/4"-wide ribbons and tack to hearts and wire hanger as desired.

Sunday in the Park with Sunbonnet Sue

by Ellen Rosintoski
Doraville, Georgia

APPROXIMATE SIZE: 21" X 17"

Ellen has perfected the ability to "let it all hang out" when designing and trying new quilt techniques. Her parklike setting for Sue includes blocks that form a path through the tree blocks.

In addition to Sunbonnet Sue, the quilt utilizes such favorite blocks as Broken Dishes, Rail Fence, Flying Geese and more.

Ellen uses foundation piecing for her blocks because this technique allows her to create "small and accurate" much more easily than with traditional piecing. Her techniques are revealed in her book, **Marvelous Mini Quilts for Foundation Piecing** *from ASN Publishing.*

Fabric Requirements:

Note: *Except for the binding and backing, you may use scraps for the entire quilt. The Tree Blocks have the largest patches, while the rest of the blocks can be made with very small scraps.*

1/2 yd muslin (if using fabric foundation)

1/2 yd lt plaid (background for Square in a Square, Broken Dishes, Tree and Flying Geese)

1/2 yd total assorted green scraps (Square in a Square, Tree, Broken Dishes, Long Rail Fence, Flying Geese)

1/4 yd total assorted purple scraps (Diamond, Broken Dishes, Square in a Square)

1/8 yd dk red (Long Rail Fence, Rail Fence Corner, Tree)

small assorted scraps (Sunbonnet Sue)

2/3 yd lt print (border/binding, backing)

29" x 25" batting

Additional Supplies:

transfer pen or pencil
five round buttons, 3/8" to 5/8" diameter

Shown in full color on page 10.

two heart buttons, 1/2" across
paper (notebook paper, copier paper, or computer paper if using paper foundations)
1/2 yd paper-backed fusible web
permanent ink pen or a pencil
glue stick
paper scissors
matching thread

Pattern Pieces (pages 72, 85 & 86):

5" Sunbonnet Sue
Broken Dishes Block
Diamond Block
Flying Geese Block
Skinny Tree Block
Patched Tree Block
Long Rail Fence Block
Rail Fence Corner Block
Square in the Square Block

Cutting Requirements:

four 4 1/2" squares, muslin (or paper)
twelve 2 1/2" squares, muslin (or paper)
seventeen 2 1/2" x 4 1/2" rectangles,
muslin (or paper)
two 4" x 6 1/2" rectangles, muslin (or paper)
two 3" x 6 1/2" rectangles, muslin (or paper)
Note: *Remaining fabrics are cut as you piece each block.*

Instructions:

Foundation Piecing

Foundation piecing techniques make little blocks very easy to construct. If you have never tried foundation piecing, you will be amazed at how fast and accurate it is. By piecing your patches onto either paper or muslin, you don't need templates to cut itty-bitty, little triangles and squares.

TRANSFERRING THE BLOCK

1. Using a transfer pen and following manufacturer's directions, transfer the required blocks onto foundations as follows:

four Square in a Square Blocks, 4 1/2" squares

52

six Broken Dishes Block, 2 1/2" square

five Diamond Blocks, 2 1/2" x 4 1/2" rectangles

nine Long Rail Fence Blocks, 2 1/2" x 4 1/2" rectangles

six Rail Fence Corner blocks, 2 1/2" squares

two Large Trees, 4" x 6 1/2" rectangles

two Skinny Trees, 3" x 6 1/2" rectangles

three Flying Geese, 2 1/2" x 4 1/2" rectangles

2. Using a permanent marking pen or a pencil, write numbers and colors of fabrics on each foundation, **Fig 1**.

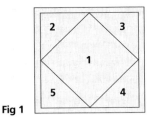

Fig 1

MAKING THE BLOCKS USING FOUNDATION PIECING

Broken Dishes Block

The following instructions for making the Broken Dishes Block is a detailed explanation of foundation piecing. Please read carefully before making your blocks.

1. Roughly cut a 2" square of background (plaid) fabric. This square will be bigger than is needed. But, one of the wonderful things about foundation piecing is that we are not going to deal with little pieces of fabric.

2. On the unmarked side of a Broken Dishes foundation, center the square right side up over patch 1, **Fig 2**. Holding the foundation up to the light with the printed side facing you, check to make sure that you have left at least a 1/4" seam allowance of fabric on all four sides of the patch. You may find it handy to put a dab of glue stick on the foundation to anchor this first patch.

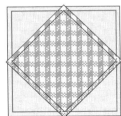

Fig 2

3. Holding foundation with printed side facing you, fold foundation towards you a scant 1/4" above the line between patch 1 and patch 2, **Fig 3**. You should see a piece of the patch 1 fabric sticking up. Cut this off even with the fold, trying not to cut the foundation. This is called pre-trimming.

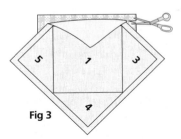

Fig 3

4. Roughly cut a piece of green fabric, about 2 1/4" x 1 1/2". Turn the foundation over and place fabric right side down over patch 1, aligning raw edges, **Fig 4**. Turn the foundation over to marked side and stitch along the marked line between patches 1 and 2, **Fig 5**. If you are stitching by hand, either knot the thread at the beginning and end of the stitching line or take several backstitches. If you are stitching by machine on a paper foundation, use a very short stitch, about 20 to 22 to the inch. If stitching by machine on a fabric foundation use a slightly longer stitch, about 16 to the inch. Start and end machine stitching a couple of stitches before and after the printed line. By using a short stitch we are anchoring the stitching and do not need to backstitch.

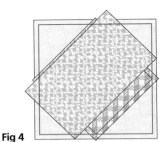

Fig 4

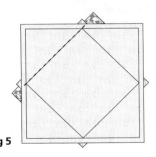

Fig 5

5. Turn the foundation fabric side up and smooth patch 2 open, **Fig 6**; finger press or iron. To finger press, run the edge of your nail over the seam to make sure that the patch is open and lying flat. Turn the foundation so that the printed side faces you and hold the foundation up to the light to make sure that you still have enough fabric for seam allowances.

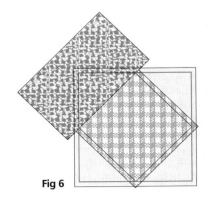

Fig 6

6. Fold the foundation towards you 1/4" above the sewing line between patch 1 and patch 3; pre-trim as above. Take another piece of green, roughly cut to 2 1/4" x 1 1/2", and place it right side down over patch 1 aligning raw edges. Sew as above; press patch 3 open.

7. Repeat step 6 for patch 4.

8. For patch 5, roughly cut a piece of path (dark) fabric, 2 1/4" x 1 1/2"; sew to the foundation in the same way as patches 2, 3 and 4.

9. Press the block. Turn block printed side up and trim the foundation and any fabric even with the solid seam allowance lines around the block to complete Broken Dishes Block, **Fig 7**.

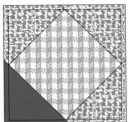

Fig 7   make 6

Note: *If you are using paper foundations, do not remove the paper until all blocks are sewn together!*

10. Make a total of six Broken Dishes Blocks.

continued

HINTS FOR FOUNDATION PIECING

1. As you are adding patches and assembling your block you will notice that you have pieces of fabric sticking out here and there. Don't panic! All the excess will vanish as you add patches and do your final trimming.

2. Ripping out is unpleasant! Well, it's actually worse than unpleasant, but occasionally it has to be done. Removing hand stitching is not a problem, but those tiny machine stitches are almost impossible to get out. Trim the offending patch fabric on one side of the stitching line as close to the stitching as you can get. Then grab the remaining patch fabric and wiggle and yank until the fabric comes free. If the remaining fabric refuses to come free, trim it off. Then, use a tweezers to fray the edge and remove the wisps of fabric. You still have the stitching but now the fabric is gone. Then put the new patch down and very carefully stitch right on top or a hair to the left of the previous stitching.

3. If you are using scraps to make this quilt you do not need to roughly cut your patches to shape. Just grab a scrap that looks at least as large as you need and sew it to the foundation. You will trim the excess off as you continue making the block. The rough cut sizes are given for cutting from yardage and also so you will know if a scrap is too small before you sew it on.

4. Use rectangular pieces of fabric for foundation piecing triangles because it can be difficult to roughly cut triangles of the appropriate size and shape. Position and sew them in numerical order on the foundation. The little bit of fabric that we are wasting makes up for a lot of sewing, ripping and gnashing of teeth!

Square in the Square Block

1. Make the Square in the Square Block exactly the same way as the Broken Dishes Block adding an extra round of triangles, **Fig 8**. For one of the outer triangles use the path (dark) fabric. For the three remaining outer triangles use the background (plaid) fabric. Use green for the center and inner triangles.

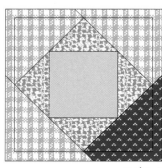

Fig 8   make 4

2. Rough cut sizes for the patches are as follows:

    2 3/4" x 2 3/4", center (patch 1)

    1 3/4" x 2 3/4", inner triangles (patches 2, 3, 4, 5)

    3 3/4" x 2 1/4", outer triangles (patches 6, 7, 8, 9)

3. Make a total of four Square in the Square Blocks.

Diamond Block

1. Mark an X in patches 2 and 4 of three of diamond foundations; mark an X in patches 3 and 5 of remaining two diamond foundations, **Fig 9**. Use path (dark) fabric for each patch marked with an X; use green fabric for unmarked patches.

Fig 9

2. Roughly cut a piece of path (dark) fabric 4 3/4" x 2 3/4" for the Diamond; place it right side up on unprinted side of foundation. Anchor with a dab of glue stick.

3. Holding foundation with printed side towards you, fold foundation back a scant 1/4" above the line between patch 1 and patch 2; trim excess fabric to 1/4".

4. If patch 2 has an X, select a piece of path (dark) fabric about 3" x 2". Otherwise use a piece of green fabric the same size. Place the patch 2 fabric right side down over trimmed edge of patch 1. Turn foundation over and sew on the marked line.

5. Smooth patch 2 open and make sure fabric covers seam allowances. *Note: Checking for seam allowances on these long narrow triangles is very important! This is the patch shape where it is easiest to have a mistake.*

6. Add patches 3, 4, 5 in the same manner using the appropriate fabrics.

7. Make remaining four Diamond blocks being careful of color placement, **Fig 10**.

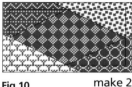   

Fig 10   make 2   make 3

Note: The rough cut patch sizes that are used are obviously very generous. When blocks have long skinny triangles, it is unfortunately, all too easy to sew on a patch and have it not fit right.

Long Rail Fence Block

1. Rough cut the following pieces:

    4 3/4" x 1 1/4", rails (patches 2, 4)

    4 3/4" x 1", greens (patches 1, 3, 5)

2. Referring to Foundation Piecing in Broken Dishes Block, page 5, make nine Long Rail Fence Blocks, **Fig 11**. Add patches in the numerical order on foundation.

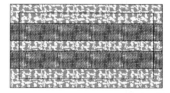

Fig 11   make 9

Rail Fence Corner Block

1. Rough cut the following pieces:

    1 1/4" x 1 3/4", dk red rail (patch 2)

    1 1/4" x 3", dk red rail (patch 4)

    1" square, green (patch 1)

    1" x 2 1/4", green (patch 3)

    2 1/2" x 2 1/2", green (patch 5)

2. Using Foundation Piecing described on page 53, make six Corner Rail Fence Blocks, **Fig 12**. Add patches in the numerical order on foundation.

make 6

Fig 12

Skinny Tree Block

The Skinny Tree Blocks need only six patches and are very easy to make. As with the Diamond Blocks, large pieces of fabric will be used to make sure that patches are big enough.

1. Rough cut the following pieces:

    1" x 2 1/4", dk red trunk (patch 1)

    1 3/4" x 2 1/4", background plaid (patches 2, 3)

    5 1/4" x 1 3/4", background plaid (patches 5, 6)

    3 1/4" x 5", green (patch 4),

2. Make the two Skinny Tree Blocks following Foundation Piecing described on page 53, **Fig 13**. Add patches in the numerical order on the foundation.

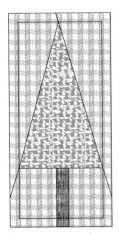

Fig 13   make 2

Patched Tree Block

1. Rough cut the following pieces:

    1 1/4" x 2 1/4", dk red trunk (patch 1)

    2 1/4" x 2 1/2", background plaid (patches 2, 3)

    5 1/4" x 2 1/4", background plaid (patches 9, 10)

    4 1/4" x 2 1/2", greens (patches 4, 5)

    2 3/4" x 2", greens (patches 6, 7)

    1 3/4" x 1 3/4", greens (patch 8)

2. Make two Patched Tree Blocks following Foundation Piecing described on page 53, **Fig 14**. Add patches in the numerical order on the foundation.

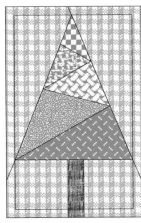

Fig 14   make 2

Note: *As you make the Patched Tree Block and add patches 4, 5, 6, 7, and 8, you will notice that you have all sorts of pieces of fabric sticking out here and there. When you fold the foundation and pre-trim to add patches 9 and 10 all of that excess fabric will be cut off.*

Flying Geese

1. Rough cut the following pieces:

    2 1/4" x 1 3/4", background plaid (patches 2, 3, 5, 6, 8, 9)

    2 3/4" x 2", assorted prints (patches 1, 4, 7)

2. Make three Flying Geese Blocks following the Foundation Piecing described on page 53, **Fig 15**. Add patches in the numerical order on the foundation.

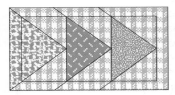

Fig 15   make 3

Finishing the Quilt

PUTTING THE BLOCKS TOGETHER

1. Press all blocks carefully and trim foundations and patches even with the solid seam allowance lines around each block.

2. Lay the blocks out referring to **Fig 16**. Make sure that the blocks with the path fabrics are turned properly so that the path appears correctly. Check the Rail Fence Corner Blocks for position and direction.

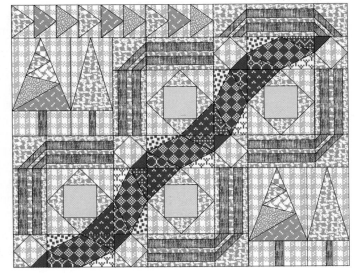

Fig 16

continued

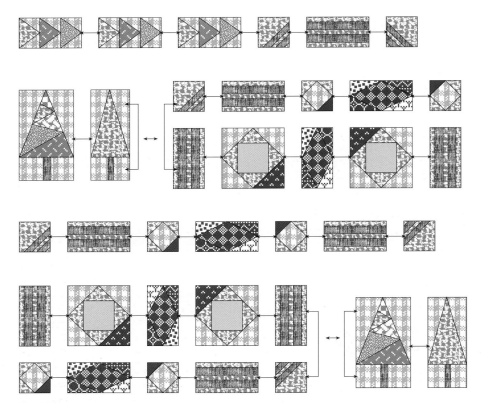

Fig 17

3. Sew blocks into rows; then sew rows together following **Fig 17**. *Note: If you are using paper foundations, remove paper that is in the seam allowances after sewing blocks together.*

4. Measure the width of the quilt top in several places (but not right at the edge). Your measurement should be 20 1/2", but it may be slightly smaller or larger depending on your seam allowance accuracy. Take the average of these measurements and cut two border strips that length and 1 1/2" wide. Pin the strips to the top and bottom edges easing any excess. Sew border strips; press.

5. Repeat step 4 for the sides of the quilt. Your measurement should be about 16 1/2" plus 2 1/2" for the borders that you just added. Sew on the side strips; press.

APPLIQUÉING SUNBONNET SUE

1. Referring to Appliqué with Paper-backed Fusible Web, page 6, trace two sets of 5" Sunbonnet Sue patterns onto the paper side of paper-backed fusible web following the manufacturer's directions. Cut out each pattern leaving a little paper around each outline. Press the fusible web pieces to the

wrong side of the fabrics that you have chosen for Sue. Cut out each piece on drawn lines. Leave paper on until you are ready to actually fuse the pieces down.

2. Lay quilt top on ironing board and referring to layout, place the Sue patches with Sue's Shoes on the path. When you are satisfied with your placement, remove paper backing from one set of Shoes, lay the Shoes back on the quilt and touch lightly with the iron. This will keep the Shoes in place but still allow you to remove them if they are not quite where you want them. Using the same procedure, place and lightly adhere the Dress, Apron, Bonnet, Sleeve and Hand. Repeat for second Sue.

3. Back up and look at your quilt. Is everything wonderful? Following the manufacturer's fusing directions, firmly adhere Sunbonnet Sue pieces to the quilt top.

4. Press the quilt top carefully.

ASSEMBLING THE TOP AND BACKING

1. Cut quilt backing about 1" larger in both directions than the size of the quilt top. Cut a piece of batting the same size as the backing.

2. Place batting on a table and smooth the backing right side up over the batting; lay quilt top right side down over backing and batting. Make sure that you have batting and backing showing all around the quilt. Pin very securely.

3. Sew around edge with a 1/4" seam allowance leaving an opening about 3" to 4" for turning. Backstitch at the beginning and end of the sewing line. Trim excess backing and batting leaving 1/4" seam allowance. Trim diagonally at the corners.

Hint: If your border and backing fabrics are the same, the seam between the border and the backing will be almost invisible.

4. Turn quilt right side out, gently poking out the corners. Press along the edge making sure that the seam is exactly on the edge. Turn in 1/4" along the opening used for turning and hand stitch closed; press.

QUILTING

1. Sew a narrow zigzag (slightly longer than a satin stitch) around the outside edges of all Sunbonnet patches. If you match the thread color to the fabric or use "invisible" thread, you will barely see the zigzag. Sparkly metallic thread was used on the photographed model for some added sparkle.

2. The photographed quilt was stipple quilted in all the background areas and quilted in-the-ditch where the border/binding strips adjoin the quilt.

3. Sew round and heart buttons at random for balloons. Machine stitch balloon strings.

Sunbonnet Sue at the Quilt Show

by Lesly-Claire Greenberg
Fairfax, Virginia

APPROXIMATE SIZE: 19" X 13"

Lesly-Claire has been expressing herself in fiber for many years; yet, she still has a fresh, childlike approach to her design work. Trained as a graphic artist, Lesly-Claire is part of a family with fabric in their blood. Her father and grandfather were in the garment trade, and her favorite grandmother was a seamstress. The foundation piecing methods used to make the tiny Courthouse Step variation of the Log Cabin are described in her book **Sewing on the Line**, *published by That Patchwork Place. If you look very carefully, you can see the backs of other quilts hanging at the show.*

Shown in full color on page 13.

Fabric Requirements
1/2 yd lt gray (background)
1/2 yd backing
1/4 yd each of two black/gray stripe fabrics (bias binding)
scraps, 6" square being the largest needed, peach or brown (hands) black (boots, stanchions and mini-quilt block centers)
3 or 4 coordinated prints (Sunbonnet Sue figures)
scrap Ultrasuede® (Purse)
scrap muslin (Tote Bag)
small assorted scraps (Fabric Pieces)
1/4 yd muslin (mini Courthouse Steps quilt foundations)
49 assorted print scraps (mini Courthouse Steps quilt blocks)

Additional Supplies:
freezer paper
1/4 yd 3/8"-wide satin cording
two bell caps
craft glue
school paste
polyester fiberfill
18" x 22" batting
thread to match fabrics
quilting thread to match
permanent marker
neutral thread for sewing machine
2" of 1/8"-wide ribbon (Tote Bag)

acrylic fabric paint, blue and white (design on Tote Bag)
small piece of paper-backed fusible web (Purse)

Pattern Pieces (pages 73 and 81):
7" Sunbonnet Sue
Tote Bag
Purse
Courthouse Steps Block
Fabric Piece

Cutting Requirements:
twenty 2 1/4" squares, muslin (Courthouse Steps foundations)
twenty 3/4" x 1 1/4" strips, black (centers of Courthouse Steps Blocks)
five 3/4"-wide strips from each of 49 fabric scraps in the following lengths:
    two 1 1/4" long (logs 2 and 3 or 4 and 5)
    two 1 3/4" long (logs 6 and 7 or 8 and 9)
    one 2 1/4" long (logs 10 and 11)
    one 7 1/2" x 8 3/4" rectangle, gray (Courthouse Steps quilt backing)
one 22" x 18" rectangle, gray (background)

one Purse each of Ultrasuede® and fabric scrap
two 4 1/2" x 1 1/4" rectangles, black (stanchions)
four 2 1/2"-wide bias strips, each of black/gray stripe fabrics

Instructions:

Making Sunbonnet Sue
1. For Tote Bag, trace design on right side of a small piece of muslin; cut out 1/4" from traced line. Referring to color photograph on page 13, fill in with blue acrylic paint, **Fig 1**. Let dry completely.

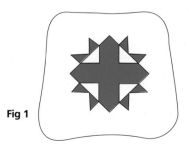

Fig 1

2. Pin 2" piece of ribbon to right side of Tote Bag with ends about 1/2" apart, **Fig 2**; place right sides together with other Tote Bag piece. Sew around entire piece.

Fig 2

3. Cut a small slit through **back layer only** of Tote Bag; turn right side out. Press, then whip stitch opening closed.

4. For Purse, following manufacturer's directions, fuse paper-backed fusible web to wrong side of fabric purse piece; remove paper backing and fuse to wrong side of Ultrasuede® Purse.

5. Draw traced lines on Ultrasuede® using permanent marking pen and referring to pattern piece for placement.

6. Referring to Appliqué Techniques for the Freezer Paper Method, page 5, prepare five of each Sunbonnet Sue piece and three Fabric Piece. Coordinate each Sue's outfit as to Bonnet, Apron, Dress and Sleeve.

7. For each Sunbonnet Sue, use blind stitch to sew pieces in the following order overlapping top piece to seam line of lower piece:

    a. Sew each Hand to each Sleeve.

    b. Place Purse over shoulder of first Sue; sew Sleeve and Hand to Apron, **Fig 3**. Place Tote Bag under Hand of third Sue; sew Sleeve and Hand to Apron, **Fig 4**. Sew remaining Hands and Sleeves to Aprons.

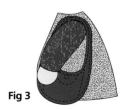

Fig 3

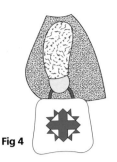

Fig 4

    c. Sew each Apron to each Dress.

    d. Sew each Bonnet over each Dress and Apron.

    e. Sew Shoe to hem of Dress.

    f. Sew three Fabric Pieces, layering on top of each other; sew under fifth Sue's Hand, **Fig 5**.

Fig 5

8. Referring to placement in layout on page 57, sew first Sue to second. Sew fourth Sue to fifth Sue, then sew third Sue to fourth.

9. Sew the two groups of Sues along the front of the second one's dress and hand, **Fig 6**. Set Sues aside.

Fig 6

Making the Courthouse Steps Mini Quilt

Note: Read Foundation Piecing, page 4, before you begin.

1. Trace Courthouse Steps Foundation Block (page 81) centered on the 20 muslin squares; be sure to include the numbers in the appropriate spaces, **Fig 7**.

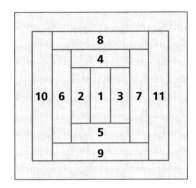

Fig 7

2. Lay out the foundation squares printed side down, alternating the rotation of the center strip, **Fig 8**. The side of the foundation that faces you (unmarked side) is the side that the fabric goes on.

Fig 8

3. Lay out the cut fabric strips on the foundations in desired arrangement. Place the five strips of the same fabric next to each other in adjoining blocks

going from the center of one to the center of the next, **Fig 9**. This creates a lantern effect between two blocks and makes it more difficult to tell where the edges of each block are.

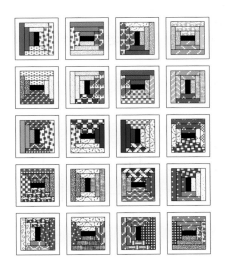

Fig 9

4. Lift one block with the appropriate strips taking care not to turn the foundation or move the location of strips. Place foundation on sewing table and move strips just off to the edges of the foundation square; keep strips in correct position on table, **Fig 10**.

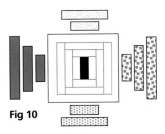

Fig 10

5. Place center strip in center of foundation on unmarked side, making sure that strip overlaps piece 1 on marked side, **Fig 11**. *Hint: Hold foundation up to a light source to check overlap.*

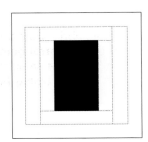

Fig 11

6. Place strip 2 right sides together on top; turn foundation over carefully and sew on marked line between strip 2 and strip 1. Sew a few stitches over the end of the line in each direction, **Fig 12**.

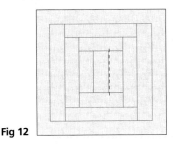

Fig 12

7. Press open strip just sewn. Place strip 3 right side down on center with raw edges even, **Fig 13**; turn foundation over and sew in place, **Fig 14**.

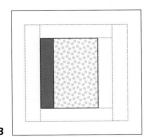

Fig 13

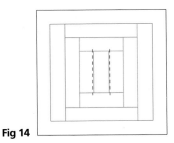

Fig 14

8. Press open strip just sewn. Return to position on sewing table. Place strip 4 in position right sides together with strips 1-2-3 on foundation, **Fig 15**.

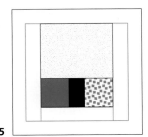

Fig 15

Turn over and stitch on marked line between 1-2-3 and 4; press open.

9. Return block to correct position on sewing table; repeat with strip 5. You have now sewn a complete round, **Fig 16**.

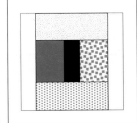

Fig 16

10. Place and sew remaining strips in order, **Fig 17**, checking to make sure that fabric strips are in correct positions as you go. Place block back in position on sewing table.

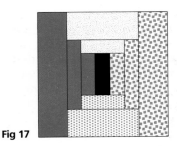

Fig 17

11. Square up block, trimming to 2 1/4" square, if necessary.

12. Repeat steps 4 to 10 for a total of 20 blocks.

13. Keeping blocks in order, sew blocks together in rows, carefully matching sewing lines at edges of blocks. Press seam allowances of each row in opposite directions. Sew rows together.

14. Place quilt top right sides together with 7 1/2" x 9 1/4" gray backing rectangle; sew along all four sides leaving an opening for turning.

15. Turn quilt right side out; whip stitch opening closed.

continued

Finishing the Quilt

1. For background, draw 12" x 18" rectangle on wrong side of 22" x 18" gray fabric rectangle; hand baste over drawn line with a contrasting thread color, **Fig 18**.

2. Place Sunbonnet Sue figures and mini quilt on right side of gray background within basting lines, **Fig 19**; blind stitch in place.

3. Turn quilt top over to show outline of mini quilt and Sunbonnet Sue figures, **Fig 20**. Cut gray background about 1/4" from inside stitched outline, to exposed freezer paper behind Sunbonnet Sue figures and backing behind mini quilt; be careful not to cut through to the front. Cut extra backing behind mini quilt to expose printed foundations. Carefully remove freezer paper templates.

4. Layer backing wrong side up, then batting and quilt top right side up. Baste by hand or with safety pins.

5. Quilt as desired. Photographed quilt was hand quilted around the Sunbonnet Sue figures and around the mini quilt. Two horizontal lines were quilted across the top. The outline of two mini quilts were quilted "behind" the Sunbonnet Sue figures, **Fig 21**.

6. For stanchion, fold 1 1/4" x 4 1/2" rectangle in half lengthwise; sew along long raw edge forming a tube. Sew across one short edge. Turn right side out. Stuff tube with fiberfill to 1/4" from open end. Repeat step 5 for another stanchion.

7. Place stanchions along bottom edge of quilt referring to layout for placement. They should be spaced about 4" apart. Baste lower edge in place.

8. Sew black/gray bias strips randomly end to end to form one long strip. Refer to Attaching the Binding, page 8, to attach binding.

9. Cut a 6" length of satin cord. (Wrap tape around cord before cutting to prevent fraying.) Glue ends of cord into bell caps using tacky craft glue; let dry.

10. Tack roping to top of stanchions and tack to mini quilt.

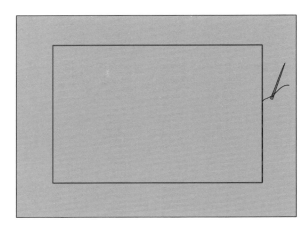

Fig 18

Fig 19

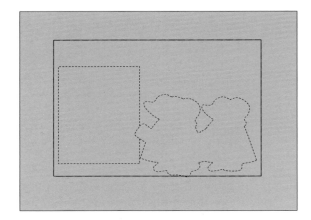

Fig 20

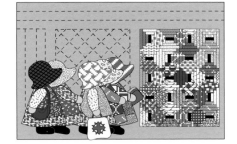

Fig 21

Friendship Chain

by Linda Causee
Oceanside, California

APPROXIMATE SIZE: 48" X 60"
(without prairie points)

For years Linda has been editing quilt-ing manuscripts at ASN Publishing, often completely rewriting instructions so that they are easy and accurate. Few people know, however, what a fine quiltmaker Linda is and here is her chance to shine. She has created a quilt that reflects her preference for soft, feminine colors. Her daughter, Kathryn, was the inspiration for this quilt and is to be the recipient of its warmth.

Fabric Requirements:

2 yds floral print
2 yds blue
7 fat quarters assorted coordinated prints (Sunbonnet Sue and Overall Sam)
small scrap peach (hands)
3 yds backing
56" x 68" batting

Additional Supplies:

six buttons, 1/8" diameter
  (Sam's Overalls)
1 1/2" yds 1/8"-wide satin ribbon
24 assorted ribbon roses, 1/2" diameter

Pattern Pieces (pages 73 and 76):

7" Sunbonnet Sue
7" Overall Sam

Cutting Requirements:

Note: *Strips are cut on the crosswise grain.*
three 9 1/4"-wide strips, blue
two 5 3/4"-wide strips, blue
seven 2 1/4"-wide strips, floral print
five 2 1/4"-wide strips, blue
six 2 1/4" x 28" strips, floral
eight 2 1/4" x 28" strips, blue
fourteen 2 1/4" squares, blue
48 - 3" squares, floral print (prairie points)
46 - 3" squares, blue (prairie points)
four 2"-wide strips, floral (first border)
five 2 1/2"-wide strips, blue (second border)
six 3"-wide strips, floral (third border)

Shown in full color on page 16.

Instructions:

Making Block A

1. Sew a 2 1/4" floral strip on each side of a 5 3/4" blue strip, **Fig 1**; press seams toward floral fabric. Repeat for two sets of pieced fabric.

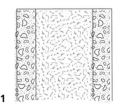

Fig 1

2. Cut pieced fabrics every 2 1/4" for a total of 24 pieced units, **Fig 2**.

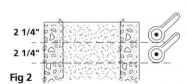

2 1/4"
2 1/4"

Fig 2

continued

3. Cut 9 1/4"-wide blue strips at 5 3/4" intervals to form rectangles, **Fig 3**.

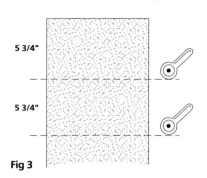

Fig 3

4. Sew pieced unit to opposite sides of blue rectangle, **Fig 4**, to complete Block A. Repeat for a total of twelve Block A.

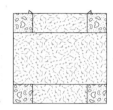

Fig 4

Making Block B

1. Sew three 2 1/4" blue strips and two 2 1/4" floral strips, **Fig 5**; press seams toward floral fabric.

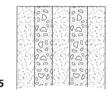

Fig 5

2. Cut pieced fabric at 2 1/4" intervals for a total of 18 units, **Fig 6**.

Fig 6

3. Sew three 2 1/4" floral strips and two 2 1/4" blue strips, **Fig 7**; press toward floral fabric.

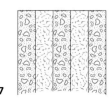

Fig 7

4. Cut pieced fabric at 2 1/4" intervals for a total of twelve units, **Fig 8**.

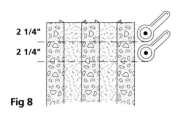

Fig 8

5. Sew units together to complete Block B, **Fig 9**. Repeat for a total of six Block B.

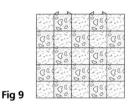

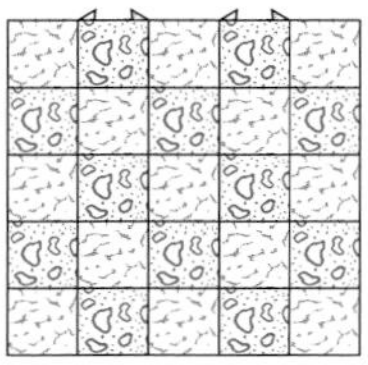

Fig 9

Making Side and Corner Triangles

1. Sew 2 1/4" x 28" blue and floral strips as in **Fig 10**. Press toward floral fabric.

2. Cut at 2 1/4" intervals, **Fig 11**.

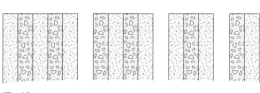

Fig 10

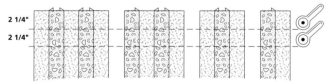

Fig 11

3. Sew units as shown in **Fig 12**; add a 2 1/4" blue square at bottom, **Fig 13**. Repeat for a total of ten side triangles.

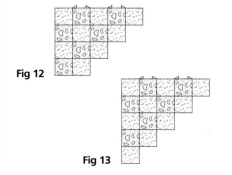

Fig 12

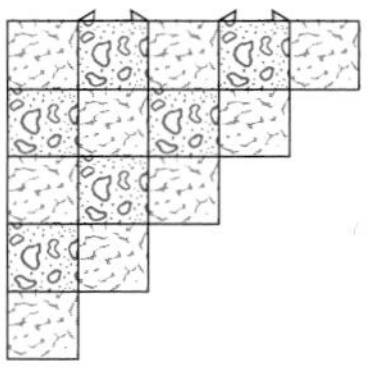

Fig 13

4. Sew two units and one 2 1/4" blue square as shown in **Fig 14**. Repeat for a total of four corner triangles.

Fig 14

Appliquéing the Blocks

1. Read Appliqué Techniques, pages 4 to 7, and prepare six Sunbonnet Sue and six Overall Sam figures for appliqué. The Spray Starch Method, page 5, was used for the photographed quilt.

Note: Three Sunbonnet Sue figures face left and three face right; three Overall Sam figures face left and three face right. See layout on page 61.

2. Position Sunbonnet Sue centered diagonally in Block A, **Fig 15**. Repeat for remaining Sunbonnet Sue and Overall Sam figures.

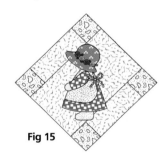

Fig 15

Making Prairie Points

1. Fold 3" floral print square in half diagonally with wrong sides together; fold again, **Fig 16**. Press.

2. Repeat for all 3" squares. You will need 48 floral and 46 blue prairie points. Set aside.

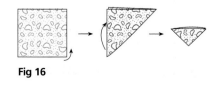

Fig 16

Finishing the Quilt

1. Place blocks, side triangles and corner triangles in diagonal rows, **Fig 17**.

2. Sew blocks and triangles together in rows, then sew rows together.

Fig 17

3. Stay stitch around entire edge of quilt 1/4" from inner corners of blue squares to prevent stretching, **Fig 18**.

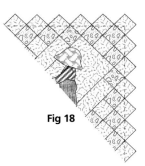

Fig 18

4. Sew first floral print border to top and bottom first, placing border strip even with inner corners of quilt top; trim excess fabric points even with border strip, **Fig 19**. Repeat for sides.

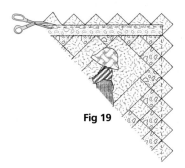

Fig 19

5. Add second blue border to top and bottom first, then sides; repeat for third floral print border.

6. Layer backing wrong side up, then batting and quilt top right side up. Baste by hand or with safety pins.

7. Quilt as desired. Photographed quilt was machine quilted horizontally and vertically through the floral squares and next to the Sunbonnet Sue and Overall Sam figures. Quilting-in-the-ditch was done in the seams between the borders and around the Block As.

8. Position prairie points along all four sides of quilt: alternate eleven floral print and ten blue prairie points along top and bottom edge of quilt top and alternate thirteen floral print and thirteen blue along sides. Overlap slightly

if necessary by tucking one inside the next, **Fig 20**. Pin prairie points to quilt top trying not to catch backing with the pins.

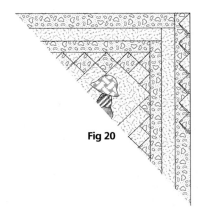

Fig 20

9. Sew prairie points in place 1/4" from edge, being sure not to catch the backing in your sewing.

10. Trim batting and backing even with quilt top.

11. Fold prairie points toward outside of quilt. Fold raw edges of backing under 1/4", then pin to quilt top, matching folded edge of backing to stitching line of quilt top. Blind stitch in place, **Fig 21**.

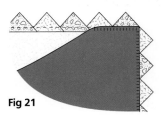

Fig 21

12. Tack four ribbon roses to Sue's Bonnet above rim. Cut 1/8" ribbon into 9" lengths; tie into small bows. Tack bow to back of Sue's Apron. Repeat for all Sunbonnet Sue Blocks.

13. Sew button to top of Sam's Overalls. Repeat for all Overall Sam Blocks.

Friends Forever

by Anita Murphy
Kountze, Texas

APPROXIMATE SIZE: 34 1/2" X 34 1/2"

Well-known teacher, lecturer, quiltmaker and author, Anita Murphy's appliqué quilts always have a warm and endearing quality. This quilt is no exception.

Here are Sue and Sam at some of the most important moments in their lives: Pre-Kindergarten Play Days with balloons and kites, School Days, Young Love and Courtship, The Wedding, and Baby Makes Three.

Anita was inspired by the memory of her dear husband James, whose spirit continues to encompass her work and her life.

Fabric Requirements:

1 1/2 yd small green floral print (quilt blocks, setting triangles, outside border)
1 yd solid blue (sky)
1 yd solid green (sashing, inner border and top side of binding)
assorted scraps (appliqué pieces- color references are found in Cutting Requirements)
6" square black Ultrasuede®, Shoes and Sam's wedding Hat
3" x 3" square pink Ultrasuede®, Hands
1" x 1" piece of rose Ultrasuede®, Balloon
two 1 1/4" x 1 1/4" brown print, Kite
1/4" x 6" gray Ultrasuede®, Flag Pole
1/4" x 1 1/4" gray Ultrasuede®, Sign Post
1" x 1" gray Ultrasuede®, Sign
2" x 2" gold print, Butterfly
1 1/2 yds lt green (backing and back side of binding)
42" square batting

Additional Supplies:

ribbon roses, 1/2" diameter
  one red
  six pink
  one peach
  one blue
  one purple
  one white

Shown in full color on page 9.

two ribbon roses with bows, white
embroidery floss, brown, black, blue (to match blue ribbon), white and orange
one embroidered appliqué U.S. Flag, 1" x 1 1/2"
small orange silk flower, 3/4" diameter
9" length 1/8"-wide satin ribbon, blue
2" length 1/4"-wide picot-edge satin ribbon, red
2" length 1/8"-wide satin ribbon, brown
2" length 1/8"-wide satin ribbon, white
2" length 1/4"-wide black/white trim
2" length rattail trim, purple
3" length 2"-wide pre-gathered lace trim
8" length 1 1/2"-wide pre-gathered lace

black permanent marking pen

Pattern Pieces (pages 72, 75 and 81):

5" Sunbonnet Sue
5" Overall Sam
Kite
Butterfly
Balloon
Sign
School Books

Cutting Requirements:

Notes: *For cutting two pieces, place fabric right sides together, trace pattern and cut out 1/4" from traced line.*

Pre-Kindergarten Play Days:

two Bonnets, white
two Dresses, blue check
two Aprons, blue floral
two Sleeves, blue check
one Shoe (Sue), black Ultrasuede®
one Hand (Sue), pink Ultrasuede®
two Overalls, blue
two Shirts, blue check

two Sleeves, blue check
two Hats, tan print
one Shoe (Sam), black Ultrasuede®
one Hand (Sam), pink Ultrasuede®
one Balloon, dk pink Ultrasuede®

School Days:
two Dresses, red check
two Sleeves, red check
two Bonnets, red print
two Aprons, red print
one Shoe (Sue), black Ultrasuede®
one Hand (Sue), pink Ultrasuede®
two Hats, tan print
two Shirts, red check
two Sleeves, red check
two Overalls, dk blue
one Shoe (Sam), black Ultrasuede®
one Hand (Sam), pink Ultrasuede®
one 1/4" x 6" flag pole strip, dk gray Ultrasuede®
one 3/8" x 1 1/4" sign strip, dk gray Ultrasuede®
one Sign, lt gray Ultrasuede®
one of each of three Books, brown, black and dk gray Ultrasuede®

Courtship:
two Bonnets, brown/white check
two Aprons, brown/white check
two Dresses, brown print
two Sleeves, brown print
one Shoe (Sue), black Ultrasuede®
one Hand (Sue), pink Ultrasuede®
two Hats, tan print
two Shirts and two Sleeves, brown/white check
two Overalls, brown/black check
one Shoe (Sam), black Ultrasuede®
one Hand (Sam), pink Ultrasuede®
two Butterflies, gold print

The Wedding:
two Bonnets, two Dresses, two Sleeves, white on white print
two Shoes, white solid
one Hand (Sue), pink Ultrasuede®
one Hat, black Ultrasuede®
two Shirts and two Sleeves, white on white print
two Overalls, black/white print
one Shoe, black Ultrasuede®
one Hand, pink Ultrasuede®

And Baby Makes Three:
two Bonnets, two Dresses, two Sleeves, beige/lavender print
two Aprons, lavender print
one Shoe (Sue), black Ultrasuede®
one Hand, pink Ultrasuede®
two Hats, tan print

two Shirts and two Sleeves, dk blue check
two Overalls, blue/white stripe
one Shoe, black Ultrasuede®
one Hand (Sue), pink Ultrasuede®

Background and Border:
Note: All measurements and cuts include 1/4" seam allowance
five 8 1/2" x 8 1/2" squares, blue solid (sky)
three 6" squares cut in half diagonally, small green floral print
two 21" squares, cut in half diagonally, small green floral print (side setting triangles)
one 16 1/2" square, cut in quarters diagonally, small green floral print (corner triangles)
two 3 1/2" x 35 1/2" strips, small green floral print (top and bottom border)
two 3 1/2" x 29 1/2" strips, small green floral print (side border)
two 1 1/2" x 28 1/2" strips, green solid (sashing)
two 1 1/2" x 10 1/4" strips, green solid (sashing)
eight 1 1/2" x 8 1/2" strips, green solid (sashing)
two 1 1/2" x 29 1/2" strips, green solid (inner border top and bottom)
two 1 1/2" x 26 1/2" strips, green solid (inner border sides)
four 1" x 36" strips green solid (top binding)
four 1 1/2" x 36" strips, lt green fabric (reverse side of binding)

Instructions:

Piecing the Background

1. Stitch a 6" green floral triangle to an 8 1/2" blue square using a 1/4" seam allowance, **Fig 1**; trim away excess blue fabric even with floral triangle. Fold triangle back to complete background block. Repeat for a total of five blocks.

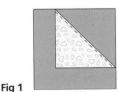

Fig 1

2. Place blocks, green solid sashing and floral setting triangles according to **Fig 2**. Sew in diagonal rows, then sew rows together. *Note: Sewing entire top together before adding appliqué, cuts down on fabric raveling and makes handling easier.*

Fig 2

Appliquéing the Blocks

The appliqués in this quilt that are made from cotton fabrics are prepared with the 3-D Appliqué Method. Each piece is self-lined with the same fabric eliminating the need for turning under edges as the appliqué is stitched to the background fabric. Also, some pieces can be tacked in place rather than blind stitching every edge in place.

The Ultrasuede® appliqué pieces are a single layer that either can be stitched down around all edges or can be left partially unstitched for dimension.

3-D Appliqué Method

1. 3-D appliqué requires two of each shape. Trace pattern piece onto wrong side of fabric; place right sides together with another piece of the same fabric (or fold a larger piece of fabric right sides together). Sew completely around shape on traced line using very small stitches, 12 to 15 per inch, **Fig 3**.

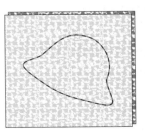

Fig 3

continued

2. Cut out shape very close to stitching line using small sharp scissors, **Fig 4**. This will give you a nice, smooth edge.

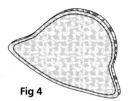

Fig 4

3. Take a sharp pin and place between the two layers of fabric. Pull layers apart, being sure that pin is not in the other side. Pinch small piece of one layer and make a snip with the point of your scissors. Recheck that you only have one layer of fabric, then snip a slightly larger opening, **Fig 5**.

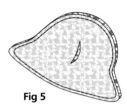

Fig 5

4. Turn piece right side out. **Hint:** *Use a surgical hemostat, either fine point or dull point, to turn right side out.*

5. Take piece to the ironing board and press on the wrong side (side with slit) first. Make sure that seam line is toward the wrong side of the piece.

6. Whip stitch opening closed. ***Note:*** *If you prefer, you can whip stitch opening before ironing. Stitching the opening closed helps the piece maintain its shape better than if it were left open.*

7. Prepare all two-layer cotton appliqué pieces in same manner.

PRE-KINDERGARTEN PLAY DAYS

1. Referring to **Fig 6** and color photograph on page 9, place Sunbonnet Sue and Overall Sam pieces on upper left background square. Position Balloon and Kite in sky. Pin pieces in place.

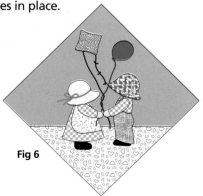

Fig 6

2. Cut two 6" pieces of brown floss; tie one piece around end of Balloon, **Fig 7,** and tuck one piece under Kite. Intertwine strands and place one strand under each hand.

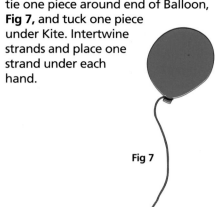

Fig 7

3. For Kite tail, cut 3" piece of brown floss; tack under end of Kite. Tie three small pieces of floss evenly spaced on the 3" piece of floss; trim to 1/4". Tack tail to background in a couple places.

4. Tack Hands under Sleeves; tack Sue's Shoe under Dress and Sam's Shoe under Overall leg.

5. Tack Apron in a couple places on Dress.

6. Place 2" piece of ribbon above rim of Bonnet; tack with five French Knots evenly spaced on ribbon, **Fig 8**. Tie remaining 10" piece of ribbon into bow and tack to back of bonnet; trim ends to desired length.

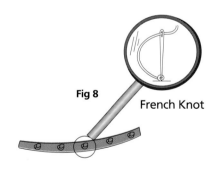

Fig 8

French Knot

7. Appliqué all Sunbonnet Sue and Overall Sam pieces to background square using blind stitch. Tack Kite to background down middle using one strand of black floss and Back Stitch, **Fig 9**. Tack Balloon to background in a couple places.

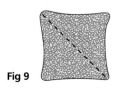

Fig 9

SCHOOL DAYS

1. Referring to **Fig 10** and color photograph on page 9, place Sunbonnet Sue and Overall Sam pieces on upper right background square. Place flag and Flag Pole on block, positioning lower end of pole under Sue's Dress.

Fig 10

2. Tack Hands to ends of Sleeves; tack Sue's Shoe under lower edge of Dress and Sam's Shoe under lower edge of Overall leg. Using black permanent pen, write "School Starts Today" on front of Sign. Tack Sign and Books to background. Appliqué remaining pieces in place leaving Apron and Hands loose.

3. Tack 2" piece of ribbon above Bonnet rim, folding ribbon at front of Bonnet under for a neat finish. Sew red ribbon rose at back of Bonnet.

COURTSHIP

1. Referring to **Fig 11** and color photograph on page 9, place Sunbonnet Sue and Overall Sam pieces on middle block.

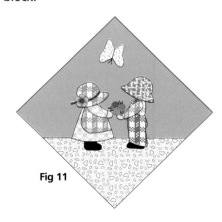

Fig 11

2. Tack Hands to ends of Sleeves; appliqué pieces in place leaving Hands loose.

3. Sew running stitch down middle of Butterfly; pull thread to gather to 3/4" and knot thread ends, **Fig 12**.

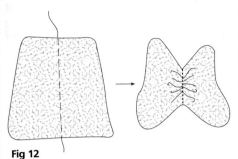

Fig 12

4. Position Butterfly in sky; machine zigzag over gathering stitches using black thread. Make a stitch for each antennae using two strands of black floss, **Fig 13**.

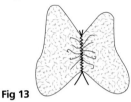

Fig 13

5. Tack 2 1/2" piece of 1/8" ribbon above Bonnet rim; tack in place with four French Knots evenly spaced. Tack small silk flower at back of Bonnet.

6. Tack a peach, pink and blue ribbon rose above Sam's Hand to form a bouquet.

THE WEDDING

1. Referring to **Fig 14** and color photograph on page 9, position Sunbonnet Sue and Overall Sam pieces on lower left block.

Fig 14

2. Fold raw edges of 2"-wide piece of lace under and tuck gathered end under back of Bonnet; pin in place. Tuck 1/4"-wide lace under bottom edge of Dress; pin in place.

3. Tack Hands to ends of Sleeves, then appliqué pieces in place, leaving hands loose.

4. Tack 2 1/2" piece of 1/8"-wide white ribbon above rim of Sue's Bonnet; tack white ribbon rose with bow at back of Bonnet. Tack white ribbon rose with bow on Sue's Hand and tack white ribbon rose at Sam's neck. Tack 2" piece of fabric above rim of Sam's Hat.

5. Sew three beads on Sue's Shoe.

6. Sew five pink ribbon roses in arch shape above Sue's and Sam's heads.

AND BABY MAKES THREE

1. Referring to **Fig 15** and color photograph on page 9, position Sunbonnet Sue and Overall Sam pieces on lower right block. Tack Hands to ends of Sleeves; tack upper end of Apron to top of Dress. Tack Sue's Shoe to lower edge of Dress and Sam's Shoe to lower edge of Overall leg.

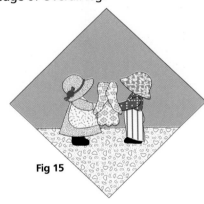

Fig 15

2. Appliqué pieces in place, leaving Hands, Shoes and lower edge of Apron loose.

3. Tack piece of rattail trim above rim of Sue's Bonnet; sew purple ribbon rose at back of Bonnet.

4. To make baby, roll 2" x 4" piece of thin batting, forming a tube, **Fig 16**. Wrap 1 1/2" x 4" piece of pre-gathered lace around batting; sew ends together, **Fig 17**. Wrap a 4" piece of 1 1/2"-wide pre-gathered lace around top of batting roll, crossing ends in front; fold ends of lace under and tack in place, **Fig 18**. Tack baby between Sue and Sam.

Fig 16

Fig 17

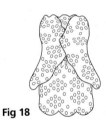

Fig 18

Finishing the Quilt

1. Measure length of quilt and trim solid green strips if necessary; sew to sides of quilt. Measure width of quilt; trim solid green 1 1/2" x 29 1/2" strips if necessary; sew to top and bottom of quilt. Repeat for floral border strips.

2. Place backing wrong side up, then batting and quilt top right side up. Baste by hand or with safety pins. Quilt as desired. Photographed quilt is quilted with straight lines radiating from the top corner of each block and setting triangle. A double wavy line was quilted in the floral border.

continued

REVERSIBLE BINDING

Even though this quilt is not reversible, it has a reversible binding because the designer wanted it to have a nice firm edge.

1. Fold a 1 1/2"-wide lt green strip in half lengthwise with wrong sides together; place on right side of a 1"-wide solid green strip with raw edges even. Sew with a 1/4" seam allowance, **Fig 19**; finger press open.

2. Place right side of binding (1"-wide piece) to the right side of quilt; stitch using a 1/4" seam allowance, **Fig 20**.

3. Fold reversible binding toward back of quilt, making sure that seamed edge of binding is along edge of quilt so that neither fabric shows on opposite side, **Fig 21**.

4. Blind stitch folded edge of binding to backing being careful not to let your stitches show on top.

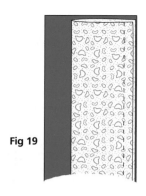

Fig 19

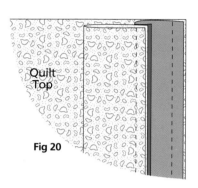

Quilt Top

Fig 20

Quilt Top

Fig 21

Sunbonnet Sue in the Garden

by Marinda Stewart
Walnut Creek, California

APPROXIMATE SIZE: 10 1/2" X 13 1/2"

This talented clothing and needlework designer has created a garden setting for Sue. Using machine appliqué techniques and hand-stitched ribbon embroidery flowers, Marinda has created a tiny pretty-as-a-picture quilt. She teaches nationally and sells a line of her own clothing patterns.

Fabric Requirements:

1/2 yd dk green fabric, background
fat quarter mottled blue (sky)
fat quarter green solid (grass)
fat quarter brown mini stripe (Fence)
small assorted scraps cotton:
  white (Clouds)
  brown (Shoe)
  flesh (Hands)
  tan (Bonnet)
  gray solid (Watering Can)
  mottled gray (Stones)
  gold (Dress)
  pink (Apron)
12" x 15" thin cotton batting

Additional Supplies:

lightweight paper-backed fusible web
matching threads
3" piece 1/4"-wide flat lace trim
metallic silver seed beads
2mm embroidery ribbon - orange and
  med yellow green
4mm embroidery ribbon - lt pink, yellow, yellow, lt rose, med rose, lt purple, med
  purple, dk purple, blue, green, dk
  yellow green, med yellow green, red
7mm embroidery ribbon - red, med
  purple
embroidery floss - red, golden yellow,
  dk yellow green
water soluble pen, dressmaker's
  carbon, or quilt marking pencil
pins
sewing needle
embroidery needles - chenille,
  embroidery or crewel
scissors
iron

Shown in full color on page 13.

Pattern Pieces (pages 72 and 87):

5" Sunbonnet Sue
Clouds 1, 2
Stepping Stones 1, 2
Watering Can
Fence Posts
Oval Shape
Second Sleeve

Cutting Requirements:

two 1/4" x 12" fence rail strips, brown
  mini stripe
one 5 1/2" x 12" rectangle,
  mottled blue
one 6" x 12" rectangle, green solid
two 10 1/2" x 13 1/2" rectangles,
  dk green
two 1 1/2" x 13 1/2" strips, dk green
two 1 1/2" x 11" strips, dk green

Instructions:

Piecing the Picture

1. Trace Sunbonnet Sue pattern pieces, Watering Can, Clouds 1 and 2, Stepping Stones 1 and 2, nine Fence Posts and two 1/4" x 10" fence rail strips onto right side of appropriate fabrics (see Fabric Requirements above).

2. Following manufacturer's directions, iron fusible web to wrong side of fabrics. Cut out pattern pieces along traced lines.

3. With right sides together, sew mottled blue 5 1/2" x 12" and 6" x 12" green solid rectangles together along 12" edge. Press seam toward darker fabric.

continued

4. Following **Fig 1** and manufacturer's directions, fuse pattern pieces to pieced background in this order: fence rails, Fence Posts, Clouds and Stones, Shoe, Second sleeve with Hand tucked under, Dress (tuck lace under hem of Dress first), Apron, Bonnet, Watering Can, Hand and Sleeve.

Fig 1

5. Referring to layout, page 69, for placement, draw two birds in sky and three clumps of grass.

6. Using pattern, cut Oval Shape from center of one dk green rectangle. Place cut-out rectangle centered over appliqué picture, **Fig 2**; pin or baste in place.

Fig 2

7. Transfer embroidery designs (**Figs 3 and 4**) to picture as shown in layout using water soluble pen, dressmaker's carbon or quilt marking pencil. Follow manufacturer's directions.

8. Center picture right side up on top of batting. Set sewing machine for a narrow satin stitch. Stitch pattern pieces to background and oval frame to picture through batting using matching thread. Satin stitch the two birds in sky.

9. Change sewing machine to straight stitch; sew three clumps of grass. Quilt inside the dk green frame with diagonal lines, spacing lines 1 1/4" apart. Repeat in other direction, forming a diamond pattern.

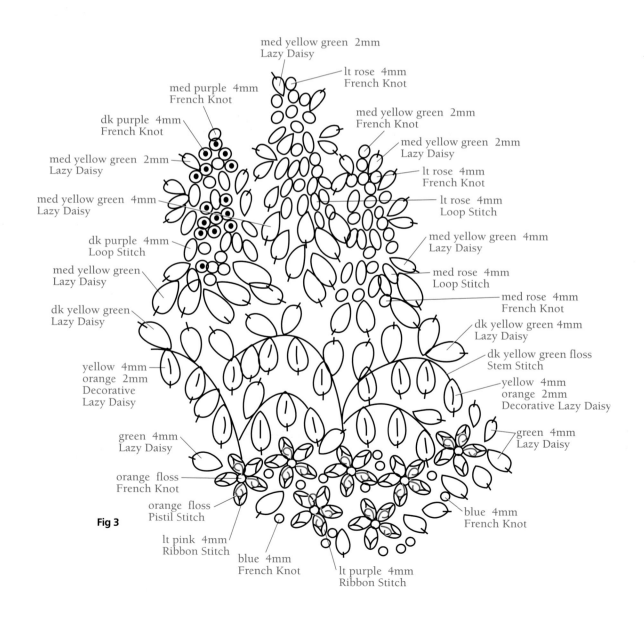

med yellow green 2mm
Lazy Daisy

lt rose 4mm
French Knot

med purple 4mm
French Knot

med yellow green 2mm
French Knot

dk purple 4mm
French Knot

med yellow green 2mm
Lazy Daisy

med yellow green 2mm
Lazy Daisy

lt rose 4mm
French Knot

med yellow green 4mm
Lazy Daisy

lt rose 4mm
Loop Stitch

dk purple 4mm
Loop Stitch

med yellow green 4mm
Lazy Daisy

med yellow green
Lazy Daisy

med rose 4mm
Loop Stitch

dk yellow green
Lazy Daisy

med rose 4mm
French Knot

dk yellow green 4mm
Lazy Daisy

dk yellow green floss
Stem Stitch

yellow 4mm
orange 2mm
Decorative
Lazy Daisy

yellow 4mm
orange 2mm
Decorative Lazy Daisy

green 4mm
Lazy Daisy

green 4mm
Lazy Daisy

orange floss
French Knot

orange floss
Pistil Stitch

blue 4mm
French Knot

Fig 3

lt pink 4mm
Ribbon Stitch

blue 4mm
French Knot

lt purple 4mm
Ribbon Stitch

Embroidering the Flowers

1. Referring to Stitching Guides, **Fig 3** and **Fig 4**, use the floss or ribbon specified to embroider stems, leaves, flowers and flower centers (in that order).

2. Thread 7mm lt purple ribbon through picture on both sides of Bonnet above rim. Tie loose ends into a bow at back of Bonnet. Trim ends to desired length.

3. Using gray sewing thread, sew small beads in arcs coming from watering can to simulate water, **Fig 5**. Sew over and on top of embroidered flowers.

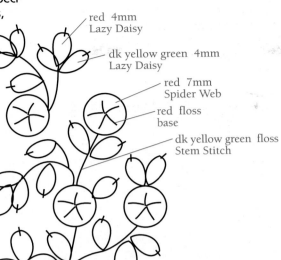

red 4mm Lazy Daisy

dk yellow green 4mm Lazy Daisy

red 7mm Spider Web

red floss base

dk yellow green floss Stem Stitch

Fig 4

Finishing the Quilt

1. Place backing and quilt top wrong sides together; pin or baste around edges.

2. Add binding referring to Attaching the Binding, page 8, using 1 1/2"-wide dk green strips.

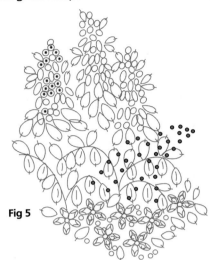

Fig 5

Stitching Guide

The stitches used in *Sunbonnet Sue in the Garden* are illustrated here. As you follow these illustrations, bring your needle up at 1 (and all odd numbers) and bring needle down at 2 (and all even numbers).

Decorative Lazy Daisy

French Knot

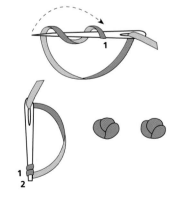

Lazy Daisy

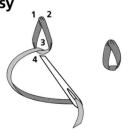

Ribbon Stitch

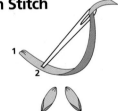

Spider Web

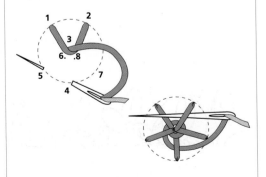

Loop Stitch

Pistil Stitch

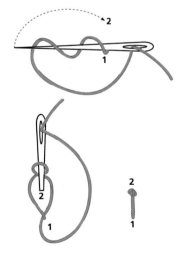

Stem Stitch

Pattern Pieces

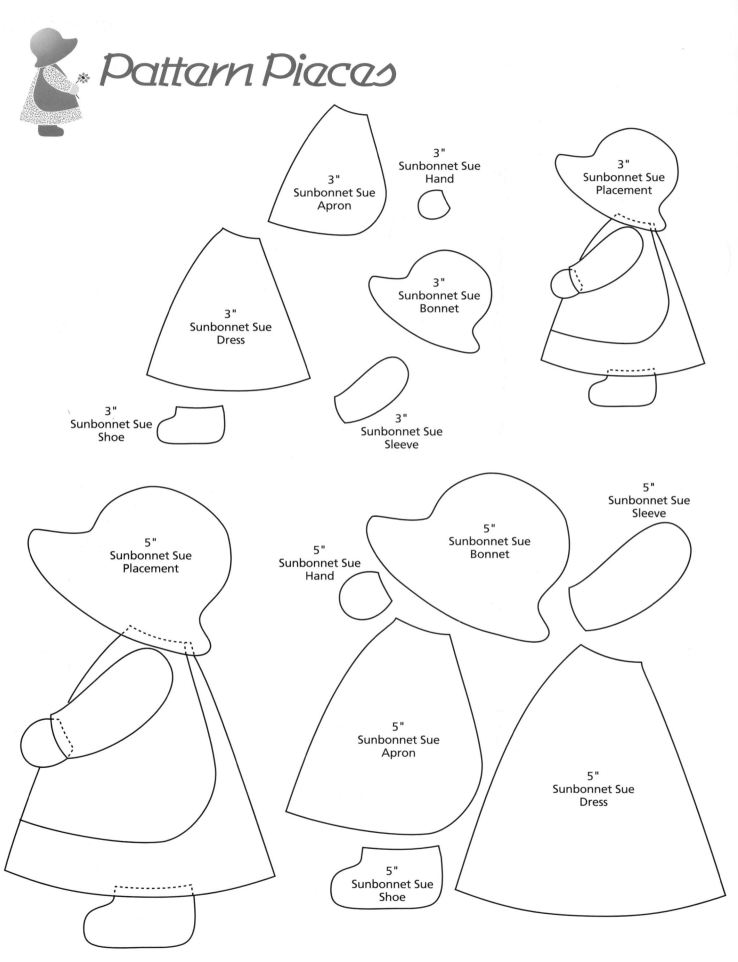

3"
Sunbonnet Sue
Apron

3"
Sunbonnet Sue
Hand

3"
Sunbonnet Sue
Placement

3"
Sunbonnet Sue
Dress

3"
Sunbonnet Sue
Bonnet

3"
Sunbonnet Sue
Shoe

3"
Sunbonnet Sue
Sleeve

5"
Sunbonnet Sue
Placement

5"
Sunbonnet Sue
Hand

5"
Sunbonnet Sue
Bonnet

5"
Sunbonnet Sue
Sleeve

5"
Sunbonnet Sue
Apron

5"
Sunbonnet Sue
Dress

5"
Sunbonnet Sue
Shoe

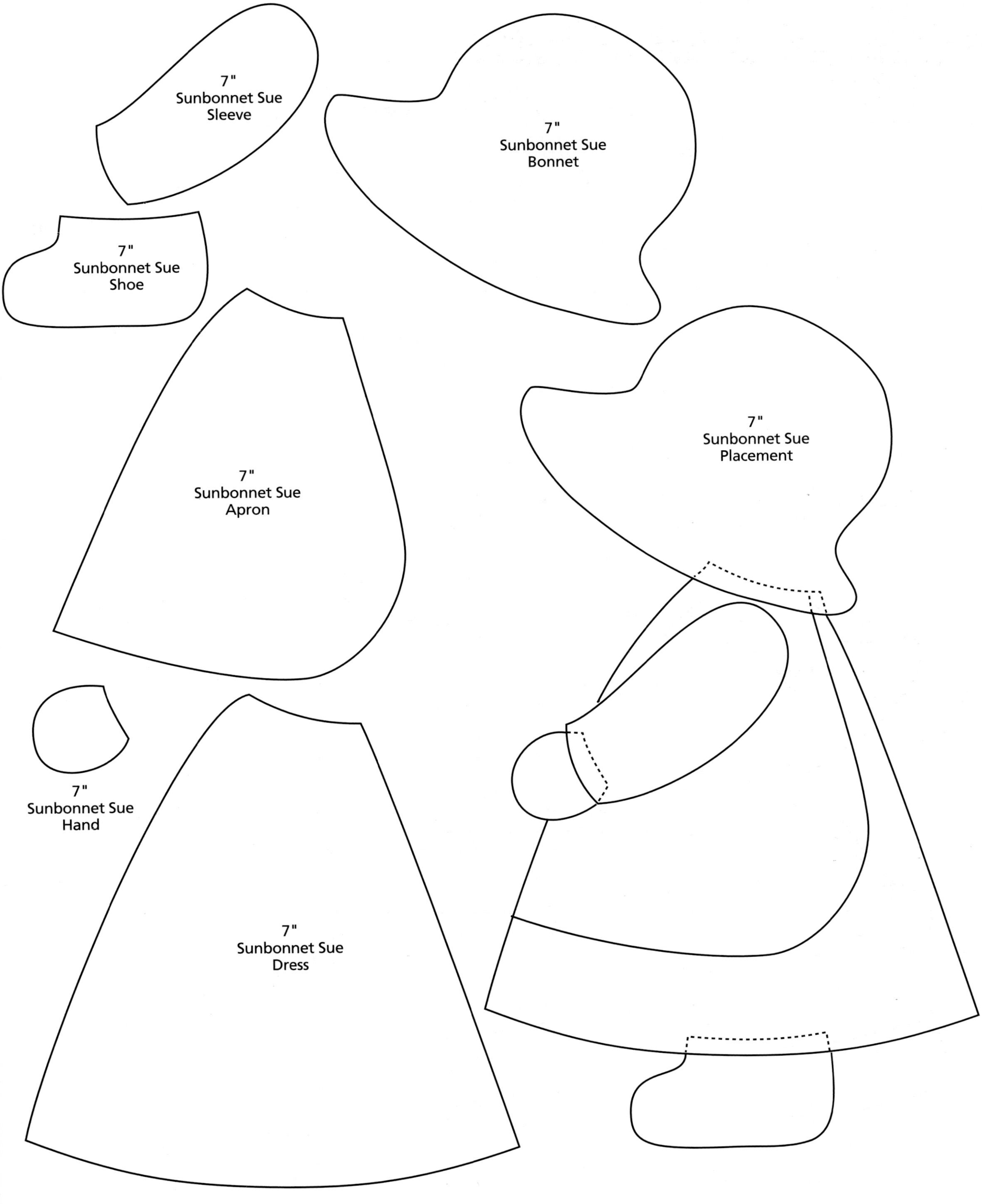

7"
Sunbonnet Sue
Sleeve

7"
Sunbonnet Sue
Bonnet

7"
Sunbonnet Sue
Shoe

7"
Sunbonnet Sue
Apron

7"
Sunbonnet Sue
Placement

7"
Sunbonnet Sue
Hand

7"
Sunbonnet Sue
Dress

Pattern Pieces

Alternate
7"
Sunbonnet Sue
Placement

Alternate
7"
Sunbonnet Sue
Sleeve

Alternate
7"
Sunbonnet Sue
Apron

Alternate
7"
Sunbonnet Sue
Dress

Alternate
7"
Sunbonnet Sue
Bonnet

Alternate
7"
Sunbonnet
Sue
Hand

Alternate
7"
Sunbonnet Sue
Shoe

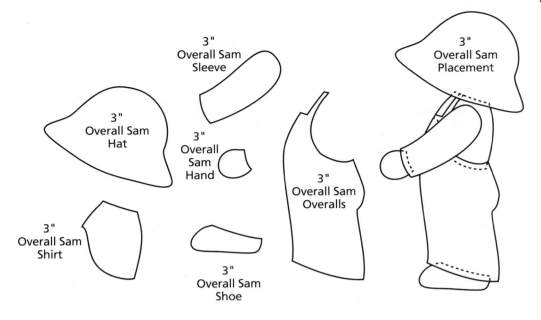

3"
Overall Sam
Sleeve

3"
Overall Sam
Placement

3"
Overall Sam
Hat

3"
Overall
Sam
Hand

3"
Overall Sam
Overalls

3"
Overall Sam
Shirt

3"
Overall Sam
Shoe

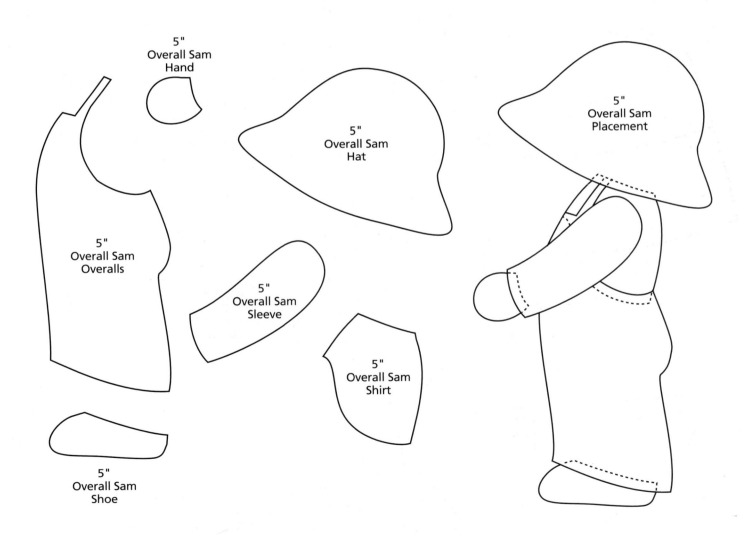

5"
Overall Sam
Hand

5"
Overall Sam
Hat

5"
Overall Sam
Placement

5"
Overall Sam
Overalls

5"
Overall Sam
Sleeve

5"
Overall Sam
Shirt

5"
Overall Sam
Shoe

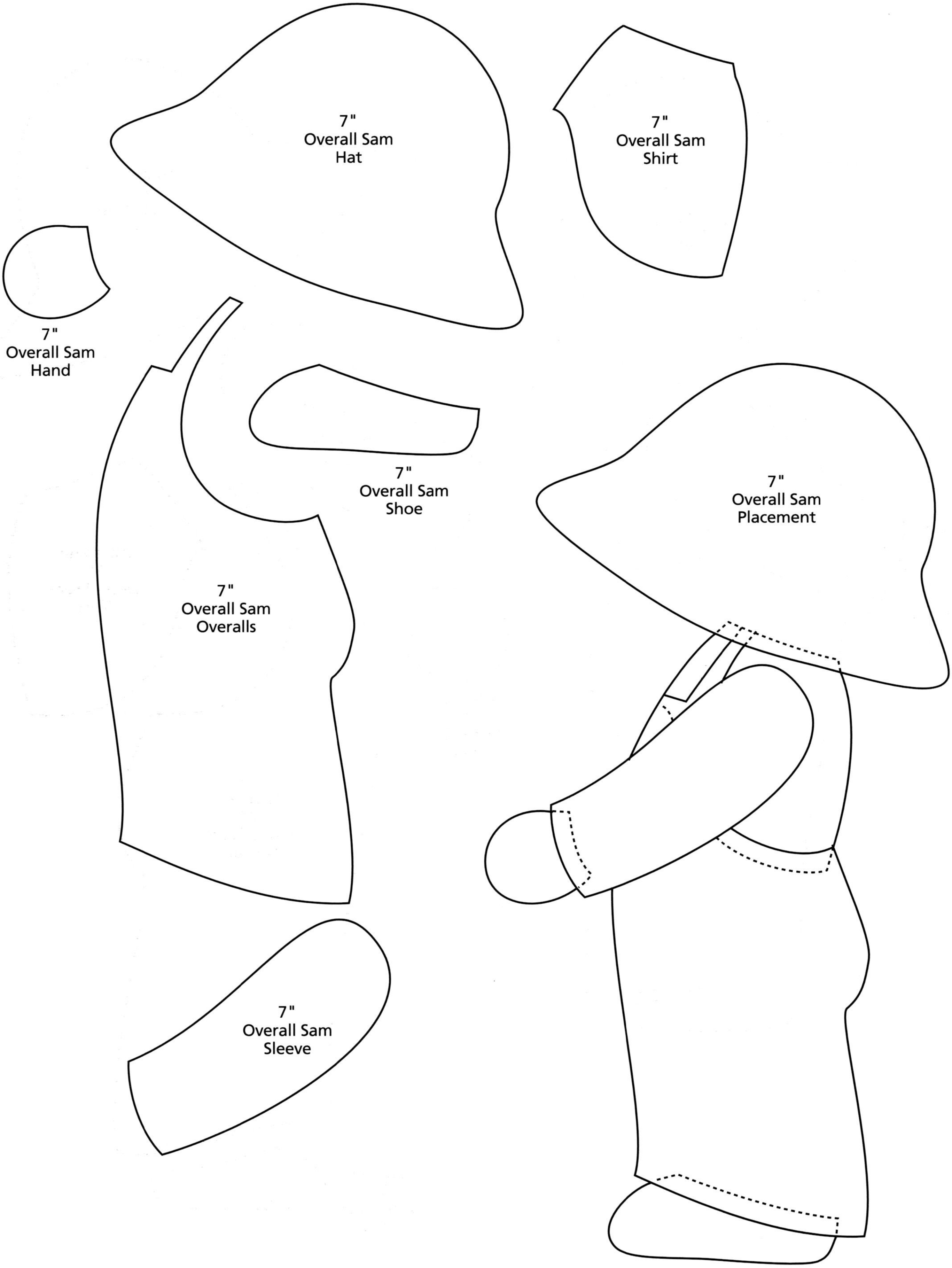

7"
Overall Sam
Hat

7"
Overall Sam
Shirt

7"
Overall Sam
Hand

7"
Overall Sam
Shoe

7"
Overall Sam
Placement

7"
Overall Sam
Overalls

7"
Overall Sam
Sleeve

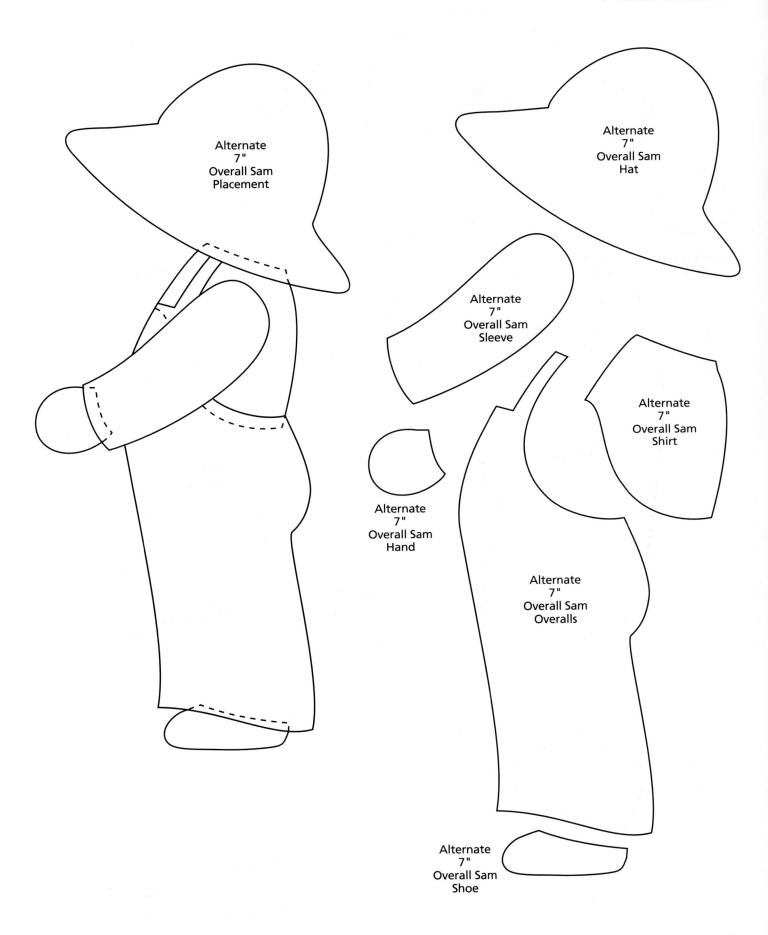

Alternate
7"
Overall Sam
Placement

Alternate
7"
Overall Sam
Hat

Alternate
7"
Overall Sam
Sleeve

Alternate
7"
Overall Sam
Shirt

Alternate
7"
Overall Sam
Hand

Alternate
7"
Overall Sam
Overalls

Alternate
7"
Overall Sam
Shoe

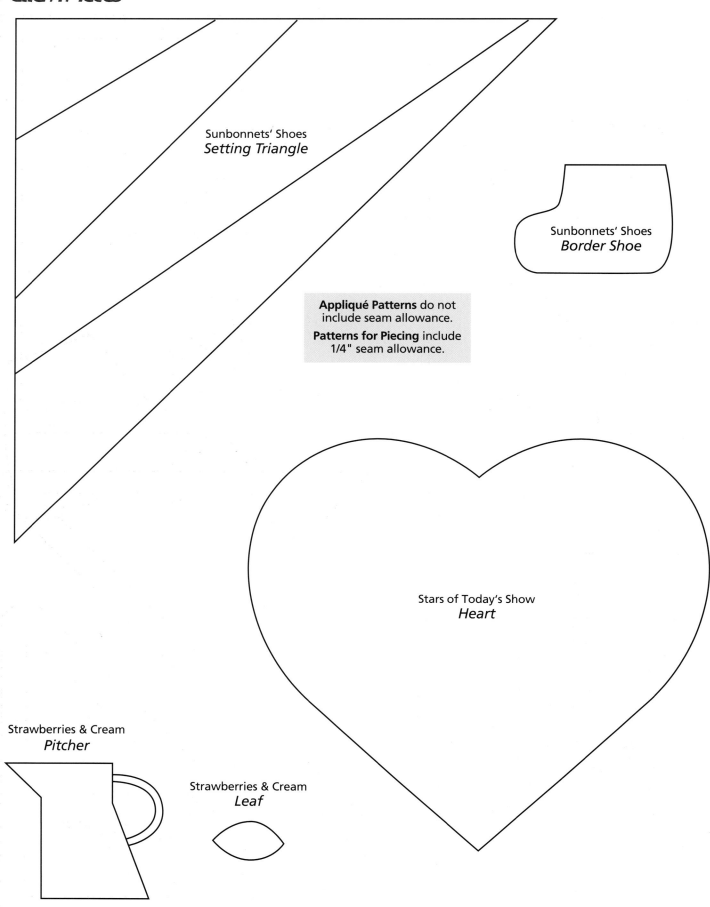

Sunbonnets' Shoes
Setting Triangle

Sunbonnets' Shoes
Border Shoe

Appliqué Patterns do not include seam allowance.

Patterns for Piecing include 1/4" seam allowance.

Stars of Today's Show
Heart

Strawberries & Cream
Pitcher

Strawberries & Cream
Leaf

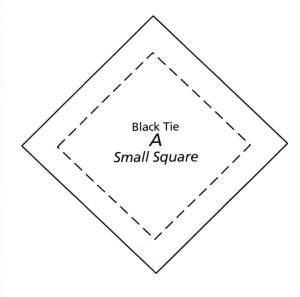

Black Tie
A
Small Square

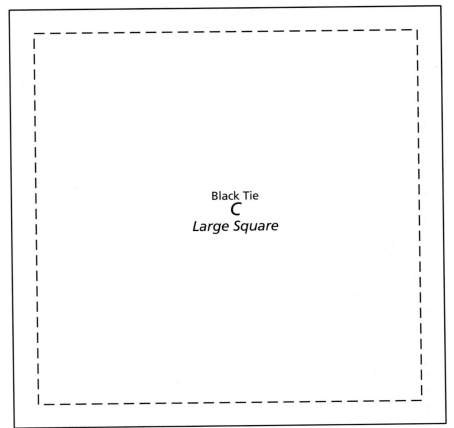

Black Tie
C
Large Square

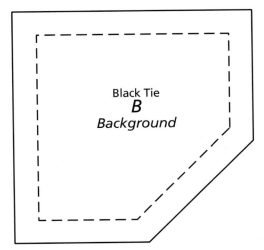

Black Tie
B
Background

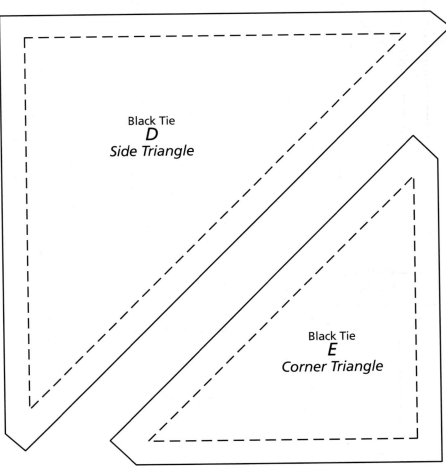

Black Tie
D
Side Triangle

Black Tie
E
Corner Triangle

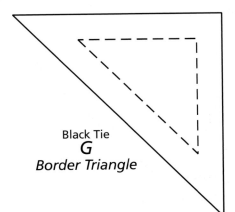

Black Tie
G
Border Triangle

Pattern Pieces

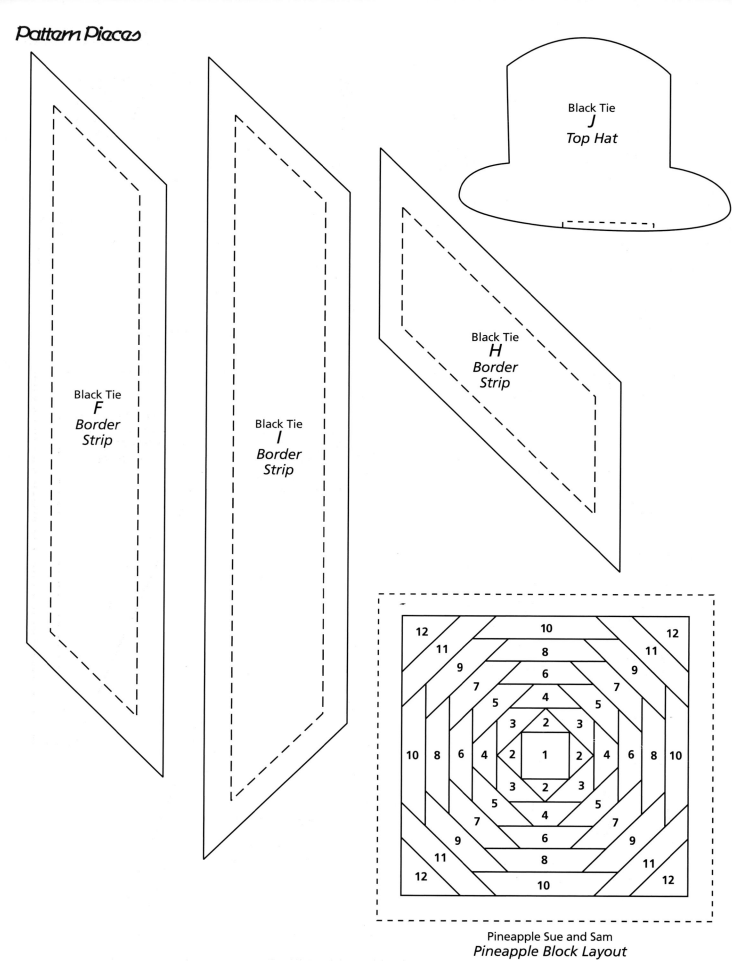

Black Tie
F
Border Strip

Black Tie
I
Border Strip

Black Tie
J
Top Hat

Black Tie
H
Border Strip

Pineapple Sue and Sam
Pineapple Block Layout

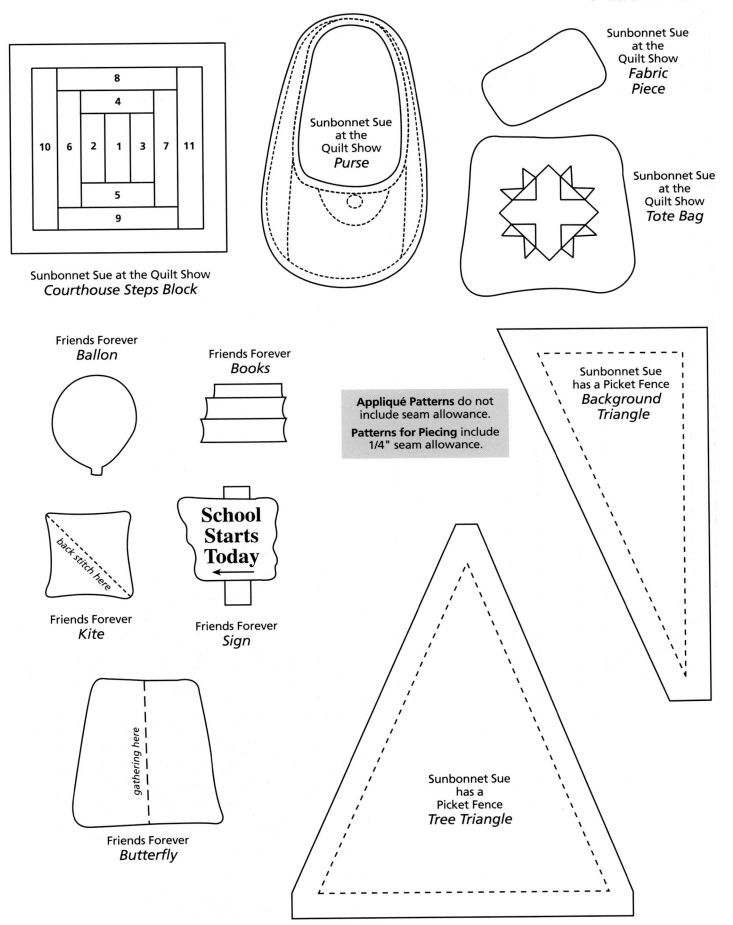

Sunbonnet Sue
at the
Quilt Show
*Fabric
Piece*

Sunbonnet Sue
at the
Quilt Show
Purse

Sunbonnet Sue
at the
Quilt Show
Tote Bag

| 8 |
| 4 |
| 10 | 6 | 2 | 1 | 3 | 7 | 11 |
| 5 |
| 9 |

Sunbonnet Sue at the Quilt Show
Courthouse Steps Block

Friends Forever
Ballon

Friends Forever
Books

Appliqué Patterns do not
include seam allowance.

Patterns for Piecing include
1/4" seam allowance.

Sunbonnet Sue
has a Picket Fence
*Background
Triangle*

back stitch here

Friends Forever
Kite

**School
Starts
Today**

Friends Forever
Sign

Sunbonnet Sue
has a
Picket Fence
Tree Triangle

gathering here

Friends Forever
Butterfly

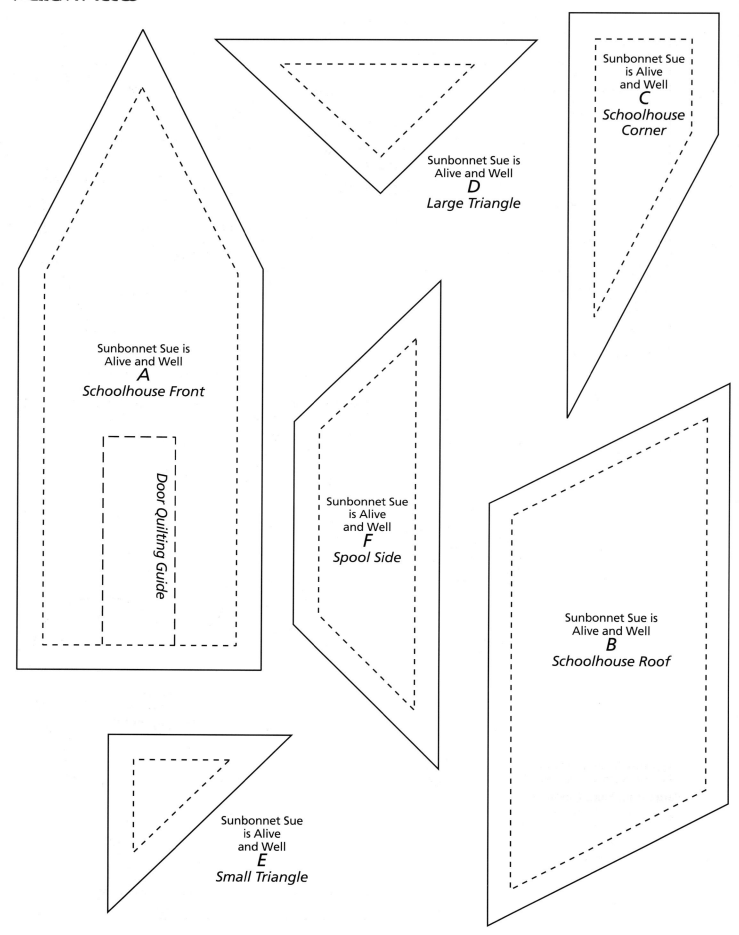

Sunbonnet Sue is
Alive and Well
D
Large Triangle

Sunbonnet Sue
is Alive
and Well
C
*Schoolhouse
Corner*

Sunbonnet Sue is
Alive and Well
A
Schoolhouse Front

Door Quilting Guide

Sunbonnet Sue
is Alive
and Well
F
Spool Side

Sunbonnet Sue is
Alive and Well
B
Schoolhouse Roof

Sunbonnet Sue
is Alive
and Well
E
Small Triangle

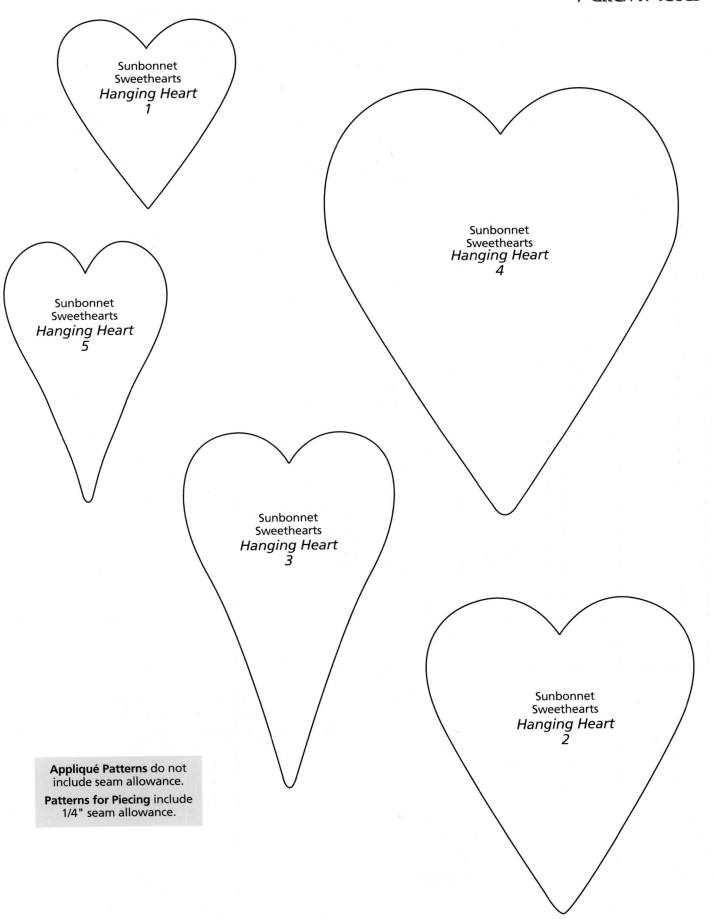

Sunbonnet
Sweethearts
Hanging Heart
1

Sunbonnet
Sweethearts
Hanging Heart
4

Sunbonnet
Sweethearts
Hanging Heart
5

Sunbonnet
Sweethearts
Hanging Heart
3

Sunbonnet
Sweethearts
Hanging Heart
2

Appliqué Patterns do not
include seam allowance.

Patterns for Piecing include
1/4" seam allowance.

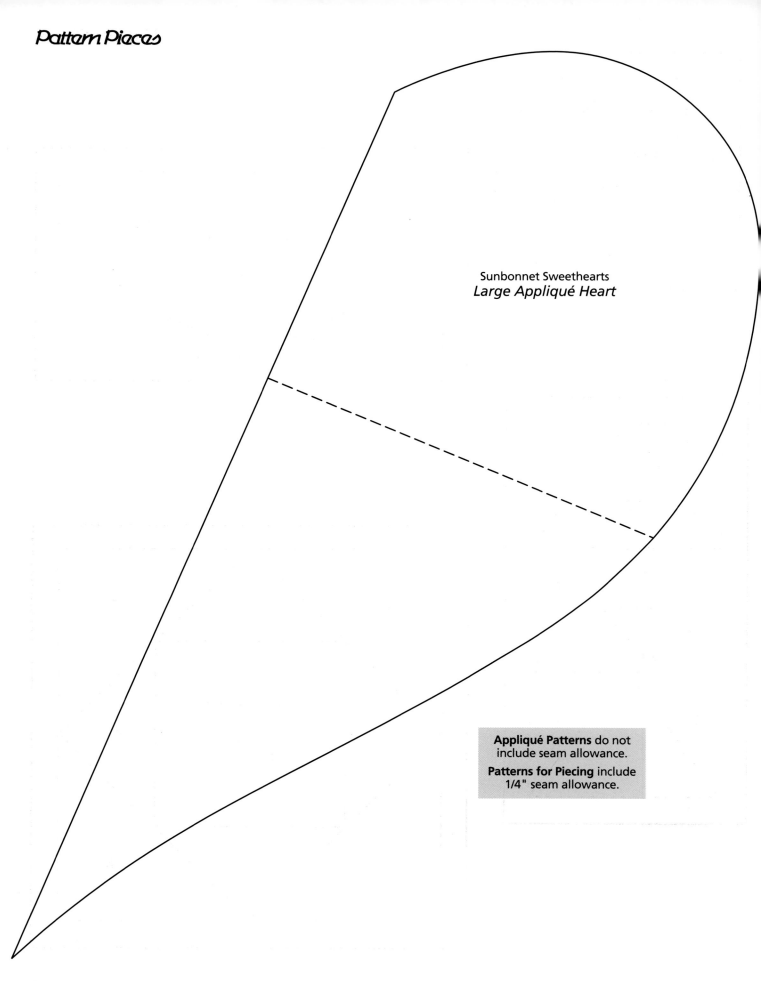

Sunbonnet Sweethearts
Large Appliqué Heart

Appliqué Patterns do not
include seam allowance.

Patterns for Piecing include
1/4" seam allowance.

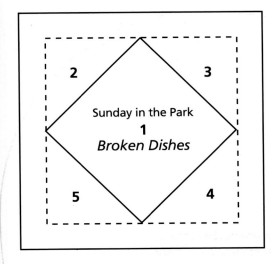

Sunday in the Park
1
Broken Dishes

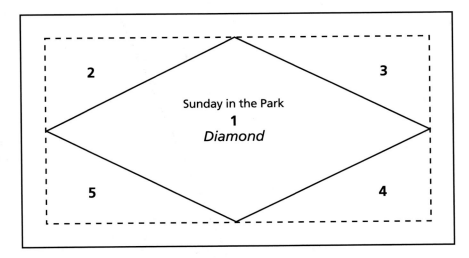

Sunday in the Park
1
Diamond

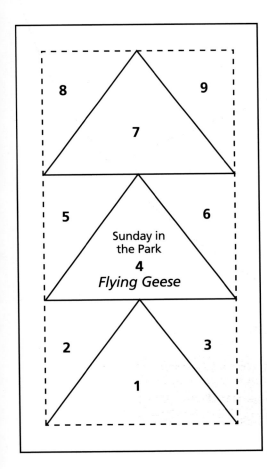

Sunday in
the Park
4
Flying Geese

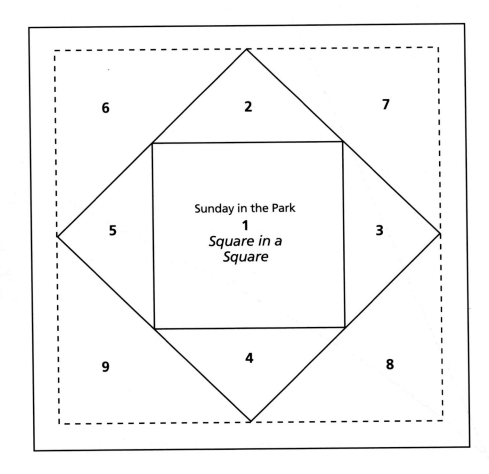

Sunday in the Park
1
Square in a Square

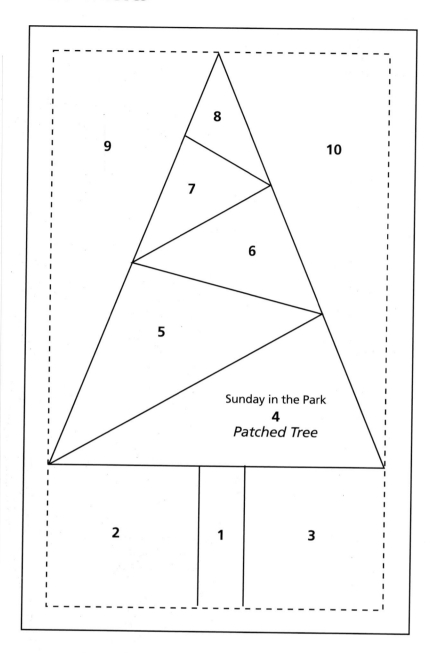

8

9

7

10

6

5

Sunday in the Park
4
Patched Tree

2

1

3

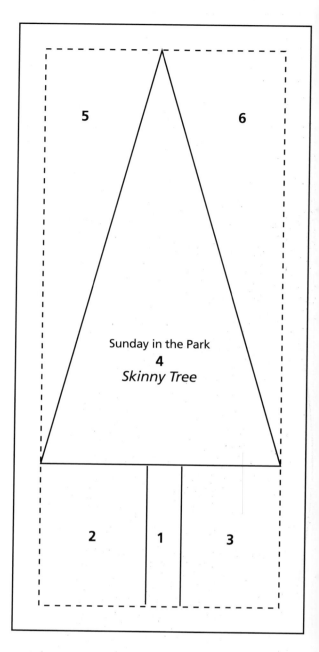

5

6

Sunday in the Park
4
Skinny Tree

2

1

3

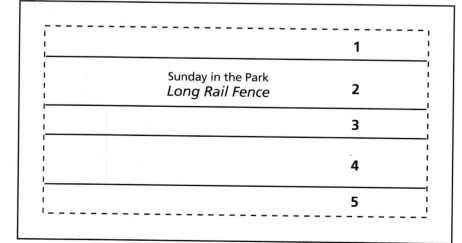

1

Sunday in the Park
Long Rail Fence

2

3

4

5

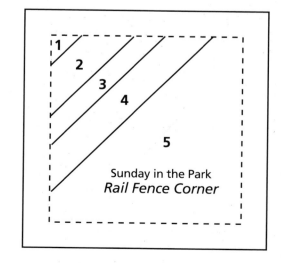

1

2

3

4

5

Sunday in the Park
Rail Fence Corner

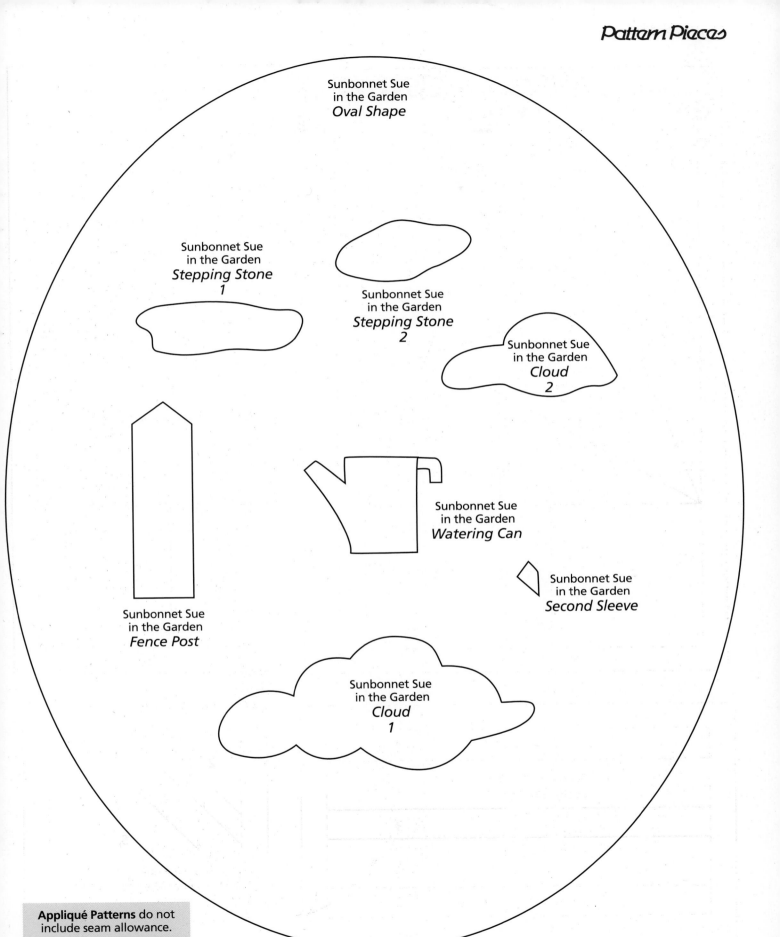

Sunbonnet Sue
in the Garden
Oval Shape

Sunbonnet Sue
in the Garden
Stepping Stone
1

Sunbonnet Sue
in the Garden
Stepping Stone
2

Sunbonnet Sue
in the Garden
Cloud
2

Sunbonnet Sue
in the Garden
Watering Can

Sunbonnet Sue
in the Garden
Second Sleeve

Sunbonnet Sue
in the Garden
Fence Post

Sunbonnet Sue
in the Garden
Cloud
1

Appliqué Patterns do not
include seam allowance.

Patterns for Piecing include
1/4" seam allowance.

Quilting Patterns

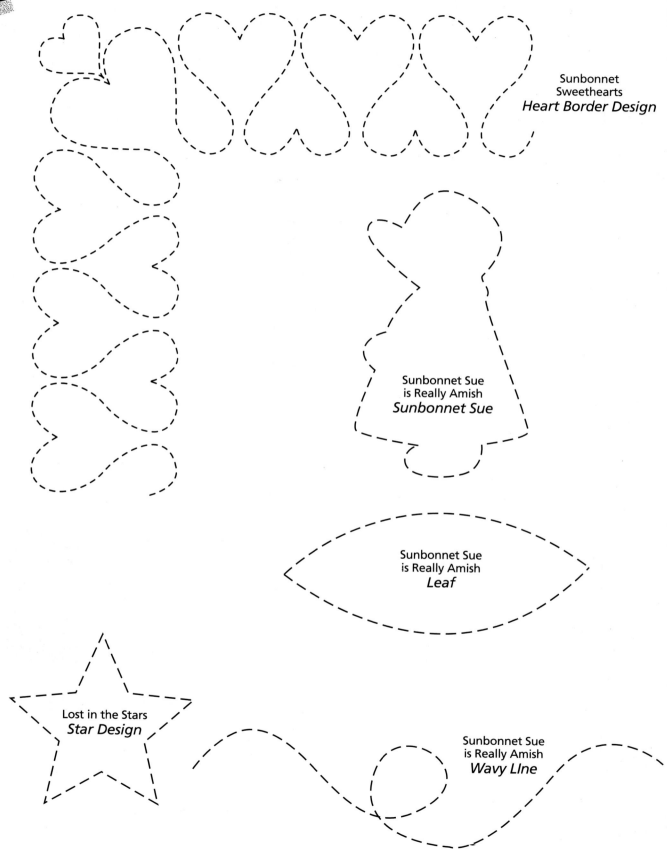

Sunbonnet
Sweethearts
Heart Border Design

Sunbonnet Sue
is Really Amish
Sunbonnet Sue

Sunbonnet Sue
is Really Amish
Leaf

Lost in the Stars
Star Design

Sunbonnet Sue
is Really Amish
Wavy LIne